Discover
the Power
B*of the*IBLE

R. N. Frost

D1052653

Harvest House Publishers
Eugene, Oregon 97402

Cover by Left Coast Design, Portland, Oregon

DISCOVER THE POWER OF THE BIBLE

Copyright © 2000 by R. N. Frost
Published by Harvest House Publishers
Eugene, Oregon 97402

Library of Congress Cataloging-in-Publication Data

Frost, Ron, 1948-
    Discover the power of the Bible / Ron Frost
        p. cm.
    ISBN 0-7369-0288-0
    1. Bible—Reading. I. Title.

BS617.F76 2000   99-056887
220'.071—dc21

00 01 02 03 04 05 06 07 / BP / 10 9 8 7 6 5 4 3 2 1

Contents

Dedication

Every spear needs a point. God is in the business of changing us from what we were in our sin into what he has in store for us: To become like his Son! As we are being changed we bring our process of transformation to the world around us. This process—discipleship—moves more quickly in some than in others. While there may be good reasons for varied speeds, I'm convinced God always invites us to a much bolder course than many Christians have chosen to take. This book is written to those who are ready to live near the tip of the spear.

In my own life I especially appreciated the deep encouragement of Art Branson, my high-school youth pastor, who regularly invited me to "taste and see, the Lord is good!" in my early days of faith. Few people are as blessed as I was to have a man who lived out Paul's exhortation in 2 Timothy 2:2: "The things which you have heard from me in the presence of many witnesses, entrust these to faithful men who will be able to teach others also." Art passed on a passion for God and his word that I hope to share with others who are faithful so that they can do the same for others. Art lives his life near the tip of the spear and invited me to do the same. It's to Art that I dedicate this book.

An Invitation to Real Growth

This morning I received an e-mail note from Greg, a missionary in Poland: "I wanted to give you a read-through update," he wrote. "My translator for this past weekend is the daughter of a pastor in our denomination. She heard about the read-through program from Leszek. Since then she has read the Bible twice and is now working on her third time through. Her goal is to read the Bible five times in one year. She is in her final year of a master's degree program in music. Her sister, who's just finishing her Ph.D. program, is reading with her at a slightly slower pace."

Greg's message was a follow-up note in response to a visit I had made to Poland five months earlier, where I had shared the principles of Bible read-through discipleship. It illustrates the power unleashed in lives when the Bible is taken more seriously and read more boldly than most of us might think possible.

A week earlier, I received a similar e-mail from a man I've never met: "At growth group last night we did our first read-through lesson. The small-group sharing and prayer time that I had planned for about 30 minutes lasted for over an hour. Only the call for food cut things off. Everyone was very enthusiastic. One of the men commented that he's learned more in the past three weeks doing this reading than he has in the past three years filling out answers to questions. That may be an overstatement, but it seems that God's Word is already having an impact on some lives."

The Bible changes lives! This book is an introduction and an invitation to a model of discipleship that has an enormous impact on the lives of those who invest in it. In my 30 years of ministry experience, nothing begins to approach the power of the ministry I'll describe in this book. Who is it for? Any Christian, young or old, who is ready to taste and see that the Lord is good.

This book has two parts designed to help you in the discovery process. Part I offers the substance of the book—a simple but remarkably effective approach to using the Bible in discipleship and personal growth. The names of the people whose stories I share here are usually their own—one or two have been changed to guard their privacy. I recreated the dialogues from memory; some are more accurate than others, but all were real events.

Part II is a collection of tools: It includes additional approaches to Bible discipleship; it suggests some resources to support Bible reading; and it introduces each book of the Bible with a brief synopsis.

Part II also includes an article from the January 1988 issue of *Moody Monthly* magazine, which first introduced the "read-through" Bible discipleship concept. Since then, read-throughs have been used in many churches throughout North America and in at least six countries. Recently two churches in the Portland, Oregon area, each unaware of the other, distributed at least 3,000 copies of the article between them. The unexpected e-mail message from Greg in Poland was a product of that distribution.

You'll also read about the fruit that has resulted from this Bible read-through method. For example, a new seminary student asked me if I was "the one who wrote that Bible-reading article." Her church in Littleton, Colorado, was using read-through partnerships in their young adult ministry with over 40 participants. She, and many others, have offered spontaneous testimonies to its effectiveness. It's the startling, self-generated, momentum of that article that led to this book. The power of the Word is easily unleashed—just try it!

Part I

DISCOVERING THE POWER

1

The Neglected Book

My first trip to Israel was profoundly life-changing—much like my experience with reading the Bible. We landed near Tel Aviv escorted by two jet fighters. The pleasant warmth of an early Mediterranean evening filled the aircraft cabin as we began to debark. I reached the threshold of the cabin door and paused, noticing a row of palms near the airport terminal. The palms traced a line to a pile of sandbags around a green box. Above it on a thick steel pedestal rested a rack of four missiles aimed skyward. I stepped outside. The nose of our Boeing jet pointed across the tarmac to an American C-5 transport disgorging its cargo to a hive of trailers and tractors. Beyond its vast fuselage stood a succession of aircraft tails extending down the length of the flightline.

Two quick explosions sounded as I reached the concrete apron at the bottom of the steps. The other passengers flinched with me—bombs? Where? A contrail overhead pointed to the source of the sounds—an Israeli jet whose twin sonic booms had just reached us. How different the reality was from the scene I expected five months earlier when I began planning the trip!

This was Israel's international airport on October 29, 1973—one day after the Yom Kippur War ended. Why was I there? My ambition was to read the Bible more effectively. To do that I planned to explore the land of the Bible for up to a year—to discover Israel's physical dimensions, to gain depth and texture. Before then my mind was forced to rely on my prior experiences of Utah, South Dakota, Montana, and Washington to try to visualize the Middle East narratives. Only after visiting the land did I realize how far off the mark I had been most of the time. I wanted to know the landscape of the Bible more than the land of Israel, but by seeing Israel the Bible became more alive than ever.

Almost a decade before my trip, the Bible had transformed my life. On that occasion—it happened on a quiet Montana mountainside in the summer of 1964—I found Christ waiting for me in Matthew's Gospel. After introducing himself to me, he drew me into an ongoing adventure. He become my companion and guide—my Lord. Lest that sound too saccharine and subjective, the experience was actually much more tangible than mystical. It was like my trip to Israel. Both experiences were a bit exotic yet profoundly practical. In both adventures, one on foot and the other in the soul, I learned some important lessons.

Lesson One: Determine to Make the Trip

My trip to Israel began as a vision planted by Ed Goodrick, a professor who led a reluctant donkey from Dan to Beersheba—from northern Israel to its southern desert—during my undergraduate years at Multnomah School of the Bible in Oregon (now Multnomah Bible College). He shared his pictures and recorded accounts when he returned. The striking images of so many key biblical locations were fascinating. I determined to see Israel for myself.

First, as a Vietnam-era draftee, I needed to complete my two-year obligation in the Army. I was stationed at Fort Myer, Virginia—a suburb of Washington, D.C.—so it was convenient to call the Israeli embassy when my enlistment was almost over. How, I asked the clerk, could I make arrangements to live on a kibbutz in Israel for a few months? A kibbutz, given my finances, was the only option for making the trip. These socialized farm communities supplied room, board, and Hebrew language training in exchange for labor. My sole resource at the time was a car that could be sold for airfare and transportation in Europe, with a few hundred dollars to spare. The clerk put me in touch with the United Jewish Agency. An interview followed and I was soon assigned to Kibbutz Dovrat—located just south of Mount Tabor, not far from Nazareth—as a volunteer and part-time Hebrew student, beginning in October.

I returned home to Spokane to make final arrangements. Then, the very week I planned to leave, the war broke out. My folks asked whether it was wise to travel alone to an active war zone. I paused, reviewing the issues once again. It would be an expensive trip, possibly dangerous. Even apart from the war, it was sure to be disruptive at a time when a job, a marriage, and a first home made much more sense. I *did* want stability; so a good job and a settled home had their attractions. And, after all, the trip could come later, well after the war ended, with more money available and my life roots established. Yet two lines of thought still held sway. If I didn't do it now, I might *never* do it. And the value it held for me was enough to make any risks acceptable.

"Maybe not," I responded, "but I'm still going." That decision made all the difference. Once I declared myself, despite any private misgivings, the matter was settled. At times it's good to be stubborn!

I need to be frank. Once the actual trip began it *was* unsettling. I planned a two-week train tour through Europe and a ferry crossing from Italy to Greece. Then I would take a ship or jet from Athens for the final leg to Israel. The war was in full bloom when I left Spokane.

In Luxembourg, where I began the European journey, the season was changing. The sky was already overcast, signaling the beginning of winter. European currencies needed to be traded regularly, which always included atrocious fees; the languages were a babble; toilets cost money and were watched by cleaning ladies; eating was an adventure; I was lonely; and the daily *International Herald Tribune* kept me abreast of the ongoing war. Some very bright folks might have stayed home!

Lesson Two: Confront the Obstacles

These travels, though, weren't any more exotic than my earlier experience in Montana, which led to a lifestyle of serious Bible reading. It certainly called for similar determination! A German theologian described his own experience in first reading the Bible as entering "a strange new world." Reading, of course, doesn't offer the physical discomforts of a cheap and mysterious European meal, nor does it bear the threats of a war zone—but it can feel very foreign. It also has to compete for time with other alluring options— friends, shopping, sports, novels, movies, television, and (again) friends. And the Bible is *not* an easy read. It's no surprise that the Bible, as the saying goes, is the best-selling but least-read book in the world. Even among committed Christians the Bible is a neglected book: nibbled but rarely eaten, acknowledged but unabsorbed. Traveling abroad just might be easier!

On the other hand, for those who are determined to make the trip—for profoundly good reasons that we'll look at in the next chapter—it helps to know what to expect. The greatest challenge is the Bible's unfamiliar landscape. The Scriptures present a world with differences in time, place, culture, language, and values. It unfolds into a disparate collection of books, poems, and letters; its poetry doesn't meet our Western tastes for rhythm and rhyme, its stories often end unhappily, its history is uneven and cryptic, and certain portions are repetitious. What's more, the Bible confronts the unwary reader with sharp moral questions. It challenges many of our modern values without apology. It claims to be the Word of God and it often assumes the presence of a hostile audience—of readers who aren't fully devoted to Christ. Given such challenges, we need a basic orientation on what and what *not* to look for.

With that in mind, let's revisit my journey to Dovrat for a tangible analogy. On arriving at Israel's airport late in the afternoon, I realized I had a problem. I didn't have any Israeli currency or a credit card—only some Greek drachmas and a few high-denomination traveler's checks. In effect, I was broke until I exchanged my Greek currency for shekels, or cashed one of my checks...and the airport didn't offer either solution because the currency exchange was closed. Most of all, I remember being tired and ready for a good sleep at the handiest Tel Aviv hotel I could find—but getting to the city 15 miles away was a problem. At the bus stop I asked the driver if he could take some drachmas or offer me a free trip. He almost laughed but then saw I was serious. The hydraulic door slammed shut in my face and the bus moved out. Returning to the terminal, I asked a man at the information center for advice. He shrugged—"Bad luck, my friend." The solution finally appeared as a gracious cab driver took my drachmas at what I later discovered to be a very fair exchange rate. More surprising, I also found out, there was no official exchange of Greek and Israeli currencies in those days!

That brief dilemma is something like exploring the Scriptures. Serious Bible reading presents challenges that need to be taken on one at a time. The rest of this chapter will point to some of the hurdles—the differences of time, place, culture, language, and values. None of them will stop the determined reader, but they might trip up the person who expects an easy ride from the literary airport.

Let's look at some of these obstacles.

Different times. In the Bible a young man once killed a nine-foot giant with nothing more than a sling and a pebble—the David and Goliath mismatch story that has become proverbial. Elsewhere, angels appear from nowhere and sometimes ascend skyward in the smoke of a burning animal. None of this is the day-to-day stuff of life for most of us. Indeed, in the Bible we have huge variations from ordinary life placed before us again and again. A number of men are said to have lived for centuries. The whole world is flooded. A man sits on an ashheap, scraping his running sores with broken pieces of pottery while his self-proclaimed friends heap guilt on him in poetic verses. The Bible, with such scenes, leaves readers with impressions of an unreal time, a world of mythic events not unlike the epics of Homer.

In that vein, even our recent historical past carries a certain unreality for the modern reader. The journals of the American explorers Lewis and Clark, for instance, are extraordinary to the modern reader as they tell stories of escaping dangers from hostile tribal groups, of being chased by ferocious grizzly bears, and of plunging through enormous river rapids in dugout canoes.

Differences of this sort aren't bad, of course, as long as their "unreality" isn't bizarre or imposed on the readers against their common sense and experience. Along this line the Bible usually treats unusual events as unusual. In other words, there aren't attempts to ignore the dramatic elements in biblical narratives. When the apostle Thomas, for instance, was told of Jesus' resurrection appearance, he refused to believe it. Only when Jesus reappeared and let him examine the wound marks did Thomas accept the evidence and affirm Jesus as God. When Peter walked on water, his natural fear soon had him sinking.

There are Bible accounts, though, that do create a sense of the incredible—of the worldwide flood, and men surviving a fiery furnace. Such cases remind us that events in the Bible sometimes challenge the modern assumptions of our western world. Not the least of which is a prevailing skepticism about the supernatural universe—an issue we'll comment on later.

The first-time reader shouldn't feel pressed to make decisions about the credibility of such things—although proper skepticism is always fair. Instead, it will be useful to ask another question: If the God of the Bible really is the creator and sustainer of all we see and know, is any of this impossible? Is it even all that incredible? Rather, we do well to ask, "*Why* this story? What might God be saying about himself if he really stands behind all this?" In asking such questions the Bible reader will discover a growing coherence in the whole: God is constantly portrayed as one who rules the world in absolute terms. The incredible is *meant* to be just that, then as now. The people of that time had the same skepticism we would have in similar circumstances today. The reason David became a star warrior in facing Goliath is because none of the Israelite soldiers had ever fought a nine-foot man before, and they were properly terrified—the very point of the story!

Repetitions. Another surprise for first-time readers are the stereoscopic—or synoptic—repetitions found in both the Old and New Testaments. For instance, three of the Gospels cover much of the same ground, sometimes expressed in nearly identical fashion. These three, Matthew, Mark, and Luke, are called the Synoptic Gospels—that is, they share the same "optic" in looking at Christ's life and ministry. Mark is shorter and more succinct, meant more for Gentile listeners. Luke's Gospel is longer and offers a sharper sense of setting and historical flow. Matthew's is more concerned with Jewish perspectives. Because they all overlap substantially while varying in emphases, they provide a stereo-like exposure to Christ's ministry.

Similarly, in the Old Testament God provides us with two tracks of his work in Israel's history. One begins with Samuel (divided into two books) and carries through to the Babylonian captivity in Kings (again, offered in two books). The other is the Chronicles (also separated into two books), which starts with Adam, offers a set of compressed genealogies, and begins its main narrative with King David and continues to the Babylonian captivity. Chronicles is more interested in the line of David while the Samuel-Kings sequence is broader and more comprehensive in its coverage.

God, of course, never explains his reasons for such repetitions, but we should remember that repetition is the mother of all learning! Also, given the variations in the accounts, which sometimes force us to wrestle with questions of harmonization, we find God drawing on our instinct to solve puzzles—a wonderful tool for sustaining our attention.

Tedious elements. On the other end of the reading spectrum from the narratives of Genesis and Exodus, and stories like David and Goliath, are the legal explanations and chronologies that appear in certain books. Some of the material is simply mind-boggling when it comes to length and strange-sounding names. For instance, a host of seemingly insignificant people are listed in page after page of the genealogies in Chronicles. So, too, laws about civil behavior are listed at length in Leviticus. Locations are often cited, but usually the reader has no idea where these places are and is left wondering what difference it all makes. Indeed, many bold Bible readers sail freely through the first two books of the Bible, Genesis and Exodus, only to run hard aground on the rocky shoreline of the laws in Leviticus and the mountainlike listings in Numbers. Why did God include such odd content in a book supposedly meant to tell us about himself?

The Bible doesn't answer such questions directly, but in time we can come to see the importance of the chronologies and legal material. First, they served the original readers by offering elements of order, priority, and significance. Then, as now, the social fabric of a society needed some public exposure in order to show how key individuals fit within the tapestry of their own history: Who were the main leaders, and what were the chief values of society?

In the theocratic rule of God in the Old Testament the key roles of social and religious leadership were given to certain family clans. For instance, the priestly families were distinct and exclusive—only the offspring of Aaron were given that role. There were others specified to carry the furnishings of the worship tent—the Tabernacle—and still others who were leaders of the various tribal groups. All were cited for posterity's sake. Thus a greater son of David (that is, not his immediate son, Solomon) was expected to be God's unique Messiah or Christ. It was necessary, then, to know a person's heritage if he claimed to be the Messiah. Jesus was able to do this. The Gospels make it clear that, despite being raised in a Gentile region, he had a clear genealogical trail back to King David, who lived centuries before. The details were important, for they confirmed Jesus' rightful place as the Messiah.

Second, the care God takes in recording such information can give us some sense of God's concern for daily activities. Cleanliness laws, for instance, must have seemed arbitrary to the Israelites, especially when they involved the most normal physical aspects of life. They certainly do for the modern reader. Yet they offer a picture of God commanding our respect, even in the seemingly minor details of life. Why, for instance, did Moses need to remove his sandals when he bowed before God at the burning bush? Some writers have suggested symbolic reasons, but the bottom line is that God told him to do it! Even today, I sometimes take off my shoes as I begin a period of special prayer. Does it make me more "holy" in a moral sense? I don't think so. But it does offer me a particular way to act as I approach God with a consciousness of his holiness. I want him to know how much I'm aware of his greatness and my reliance on him. Shoe removal helps me do something tangible as I think of such things.

Thus, the "tedious" content of the Bible has importance even when we don't see any immediate application for our present circumstances. Still, the best advice for a first-time reading of the Bible is to skim the legal and genealogical sections. Sometime, in a later reading, you'll be better prepared to appreciate the patterns and values being offered there.

Different places and cultures. Another difficulty for the modern reader is the experience of finding strange places and cultures in the Bible. When the Bible describes Moses in the Sinai or the travels of Jesus around the Galilee, we may have seen those places already in a *National Geographic* magazine, but they still remain a bit mysterious. Yet in most cases the Bible writers assume you know the locations they mention, or that you recognize topography, distance, historical significance, and so on. Why, for instance, was Jesus hot and tired by the time he arrived at Sychar and met the Samaritan woman at the well? (see John 4:6-7). When the woman spoke of "this mountain," what was she talking about?

This aspect of Bible reading is a blind spot for modern readers at times, yet it is not insurmountable. Everyone has to endure at least some measure of ignorance as they read—whether in a textbook or in a novel—but as they keep reading they gradually accumulate more and more data. Entering the world of the Bible, then, is a bit like moving to a new neighborhood. When you move, it's unlikely that you'll memorize all the local streets from a map before you make your first trip from home. Instead, you learn the roads one at a time, beginning with the routes to work, to the grocery store, to the library, and so on. Eventually, you gain a clear sense of where things are. That's the best way to get to know the Bible. Just keep reading.

The 1973 trip opened my eyes to the challenge of responding to a dramatically different culture. I quickly adjusted to Israel as I had to Europe—it differed from home but only by degree. The world, however, changed in kind when I first walked through the Damascus Gate into the Old City of Jerusalem. The sounds, smells, sizes, language, and intensity were no longer Western but Eastern—and all this change occurred within a distance of 20 feet. I began to see how the Bible described the world of Old Jerusalem far more than it did the world of modern Jerusalem. The former is busy with small shops, open-air goods, haggling over prices, and the sense that things have been this way for centuries!

The Bible, then, can be an altogether different world, especially the Old Testament. In the second book of the Old Testament—Exodus—the reader begins to encounter the biblical cultus. Despite its ominous sound, *cultus* is just a technical term for the set of ceremonies that define a given religion—particularly the rituals and principles that guide practitioners as they approach their god. In the Bible we discover the one *true* form of worship. Yahweh, the living God of Israel and creator of the cosmos, directs his people to engage in a wide range of activities in order to address their sin.

Sin, beginning with Adam and Eve, alienated all humanity from God because sin captured the hearts of all Adam's offspring. The instructions given in Exodus, Leviticus, and Numbers set out God's plan to restore humanity to himself—to as many as receive his love, believing in him as their personal God. This plan involved the Tabernacle—the specially designed tent in which God agreed to live on earth. It held special furnishings, including a lampstand, a table for daily bread, an incense altar, and a throne atop a golden box placed behind a curtain. Outside the Tabernacle were placed a large altar for burning sacrificial animals and a bronze laver filled with water.

All this will certainly strike the first-time reader as novel, if not weird! Yet all of it represents a striking message from God: all sin is punishable by death; death is represented by shed blood; and animals are used to represent a temporary stopgap in the shedding of their blood as they take the place of God's people in receiving God's judgment. In ancient Israel, the priests sacrificed animals in accord with God's instructions, and once a year the main priest entered the curtained throne room and sprinkled blood before God as a national acknowledgment of sin and a confidence that God had provided forgiveness.

My culture shock in visiting Old Jerusalem was probably nothing in comparison to a first-time reader's exposure to the biblical cultus. This is especially true in a day when the idea of bloody sacrifices of animals is utterly foreign to our Western sensibilities. However, certain insights should be kept in mind as we read. First of all, the shed blood is *meant* to shock us. By it, God reminds us that our sin is much more damaging to us and offensive to God than we realize. The fact that God demands death in order to address the problem of human sin escalates the seriousness of the issue. Then, after reading of animal deaths for dozens, if not hundreds of pages, we find that the New Testament states the obvious (in the book of Hebrews): Animal deaths *aren't* commensurate to a human death. We also find an even greater surprise—namely, that God came to earth in the person of Jesus to be a sacrificial lamb for us. Second, we need to see ourselves as just one generation out of many hundreds to have read this message. Despite the elements of the Bible that may seem strange or foreign to us, those same elements have been effective in God's work of changing lives for thousands of years.

A God who punishes. One of the startling moments in Bible reading comes when we find God willing to destroy all of humanity, excepting Noah's clan, by the flood. And later, in Deuteronomy, God orders all of the Amorites and other national groups in Canaan to be destroyed. That included the women and children.

It is these and other similar acts of judgment that have led some to claim that the God of the Old Testament is a God of wrath, while in the New Testament we find a God of mercy revealed in Christ. Christ *did* teach us to offer mercy, of course, and—even more dramatically, he displayed it—he absorbed our own sins on the cross rather than allowing us the punishment we deserved. Yet in the book of Revelation we see Christ returning to earth in the role of a conquering king, decimating his enemies.

The fact is that the Bible presents God as an opponent to all who insist upon remaining independent from him.

He is God, and insists that every knee will bow and every tongue will confess that he is Lord. The experience of life in our present existence, then, is just one of clarifying where we stand with him. God warns us of pending judgment, but offers us his love, mercy, and forgiveness in Christ. If his grace is despised, he unleashes his wrath. Sometimes it comes in dramatic judgments, such as the genocidal warfare unleashed against the Canaanites; sometimes it is deferred until the coming Day of Judgment—when those who prefer rebellion against God in this life will meet him face-to-face to explain their choice.

God's wrath, the Bible makes clear, comes only after remarkable measures of patience. The judgment against the Amorites in Canaan, for instance, was delayed 400 years because, as God told Abraham, their sins were "not yet complete" (Genesis 15:16). By the time Joshua and Israel invaded the region we find a picture of this corruption when, in Numbers 21–25, the Amorite people living in Moab refused to let Israel pass through their land. Unable to stop Israel militarily, they hired Balaam to curse them. When that failed, they sent their daughters into the Israelite camp in an attempt to seduce the sons of the Israelite leaders—in hopes, it seems, of drawing the two cultures together despite their differences of worship and ethics. This effort was a final straw in God's eyes. The corruption of the Amorites was complete and God refused to spare them any longer. But it took more than 400 years to reach that point.

God knows that corruption—if it isn't confronted—spreads within cultures, until a culture is so decayed as to be beyond any openness to his gracious initiatives. The world before Noah's time, for instance, was fascinated with violence and couldn't think of anything apart from violence—despite Noah's warnings to them as a "preacher of righteousness." Judgment followed. These episodes are brought up in New Testament books like 2 Peter and Jude as warnings against moral carelessness—reminding us that God not only loves, but he will also confront all those who despise him despite his kind patience.

Different language and values. The terminology of the Bible is also a bit strange. For most of us the biblical language of curses, covenants, baptisms, repentance, and resurrections will be unfamiliar. We might recognize the words in themselves, but it won't be clear at first what their precise meaning is, or how they fit together in a larger discussion.

In fact, many of the biblical discussions presume a fair level of prior knowledge, shared assumptions, and common values. The question, for instance, of how one is justified by faith through trusting in Christ's righteousness rather than in our own. This will seem odd if a reader doesn't understand the biblical idea of sin as a pervasive human problem—a rebellion against God that everyone shares. Instead, the reader might assume that *most* people are relatively righteous. We know of exceptions, of course, but as a rule we're good, solid citizens; and so are our friends and neighbors. We'll make the occasional mistake, of course, but who doesn't? The net result, then, is that the Bible seems foreign to us when it continually addresses problems we don't believe we have.

Another of the Bible assumptions is that the supernatural world is very real and active. We might approve of the idea in principle. In fact, the promised reality of God and his angels might be the very reason for our interest in the Bible and the world of religion. The problem, however, comes in the practical application of that possibility. When the Bible talks about miracles such as healings, resurrections, and exorcisms, we're left to wonder how that relates to today. We may be sympathetic but we're also skeptical, given our personal experiences. That is, most of us have prayed for a dear friend or close relative who was facing a divorce, struggling with alcoholism, or threatened by cancer. Pray as hard as we might, we found it didn't really seem to make a difference—the divorce went through, the addiction continued, and the cancer was something the doctors were left to address.

The medical issues, in particular, point to our prayers for healing while we actually trust our medicines. In fact, we're so saturated with a scientific culture that insists on rational cause-and-effect solutions that the idea of supernatural interventions by God becomes something of a "backstop." Praying for cancer is fine but the real solution, if there is one, will be radiation treatments and chemotherapy. God is left to fit into the gaps that science can't overcome just yet. The Bible, then, can seem very foreign with its strong supernaturalism as we live day to day in a profoundly nonsupernatural, and sometimes antisupernatural, modern age.

The differences between the natural and supernatural worlds are crucial, of course. God is alive and well. He rules the heavens and the earth, the visible and invisible realities. The Bible is the main bridge between these realities. Our problem is that we live in—and rely on—the visible, tangible world without quite knowing what to make of the invisible counterpart. It's easy to depend on the empirical sciences as more trustworthy. Yet God rules both worlds.

God's rule introduces the most basic question of differing values as we explore the Bible—the moral dimension. The Bible, we discover again and again, confronts us with our autonomy. Rather than affirm our independence, God continually invites readers to live a life of dependent faith, a faith that looks to his Word in the full range of life's decisions. As one of my early Bible-reading mentors pointed out, when the Bible seems strangest to us, it's almost always when repentance—a change of heart and mind on our part—is needed to really grasp and appreciate the message. Until that occurs it's hard to even *want* to read the Bible. It's a miracle that anyone does.

The difficulties, then, are daunting, and the comforts of "staying home"—well away from the lands of the Bible—are many and alluring. For the reader who is challenged to move ahead, this book will describe the landscape of the Bible. You may also want to consider making the trip in tandem with others. Companionship is enormously helpful. But what first needs to be addressed is motivation. What makes someone decide to make such a trip? That crucial question is the subject of the next chapter.

2

Why Read the Bible?

I left the youth hostel at the base of Masada early in the morning, before sunrise. Three of us planned to hike up the "snakepath" on the east side of this famous mesa in Israel. It was here, almost 2,000 years ago, that about 1,000 Jewish nationalists committed suicide rather than surrender to the Roman army that surrounded them. The remnants of the Roman siege wall and fortifications built around Masada are still in place. We climbed the steep, rugged path early to avoid the coming heat of the day. Masada is near the Dead Sea in the arid Judean desert—not a place to visit without lots of water and opportunities to find shade.

Water was a problem for Masada from the beginning. It was originally built as a fortified retreat center by Herod the Great. This was the same Herod who rebuilt the Temple in Jerusalem, constructed an artificial harbor at Caesarea, and tried to kill Jesus when he heard that an infant king had been born in Bethlehem. Herod was paranoid, afraid someone would treat him the way he treated others! So the fortress-palace he built at Masada was meant to resist any attacks that might arise against him. It offered a large plateau surrounded by sheer drops in all directions. Climbing the clifflike east face of Masada during our morning hike convinced our little group that any invaders would have had a problem! But Masada's vulnerability was obvious. It lacked any water supply except for rare desert rainfalls. Without water a siege of Masada would guarantee surrender in days. To solve this problem, Herod's engineers built a complex set of channels to carry the local rainfall into a set of water storage cisterns carved into the rocky surface of Masada.

We arrived at the top of the mountain just in time for the sunrise. In the course of our tour we visited the largest of Herod's cisterns. It was a huge room, now empty, the size of a modest four-story building. The walls had been coated with a lime plaster, and the cistern, if it were filled, could serve the population of Masada for months. The quality of the water, of course, would leave much to be desired—with the collective debris of rainy desert run-off, and the lack of any outlet. The water would have been stagnant and murky, enough for basic needs and nothing more. Seeing Herod's great, empty cisterns reminded me of a statement I had read in Jeremiah: "'Be appalled, O heavens, at this, and shudder, be very desolate,' declares the LORD. 'For My people have committed two evils: They have forsaken Me, the fountain of living waters, to hew for themselves cisterns, broken cisterns that can hold no water'" (Jeremiah 2:12-13 NIV).

God's people, it seems, were like Herod and his engineers. They were industrious rock carvers. But Jeremiah's audience had no hope of success. They were endeavoring to satisfy their soul-thirst by working hard in man-made business, religious, and social activities, hoping for a runoff that could be gathered in their spiritual cisterns. However, these cisterns were being carved in stone so badly cracked that they would never hold any water. To the amazement of the heavenly hosts, the religious rock carvers seemed not to notice the futility of their foolish efforts.

In Jeremiah's imagery, the alternative to a broken cistern is "the spring of living waters" which is God himself! This imagery of living water would have been especially meaningful for travelers in Israel during Jeremiah's day, for it refers to fresh water from a spring, rather than standing water that can become stagnant. In the northern part of Israel, just inside the modern Syrian border, is the chief headwater of the Jordan River. The Banias Springs— near ancient Caesarea Philippi, where Jesus took his disciples and where Peter confessed Jesus as the Messiah—are a special treat to visit. Clear, pure water gushes out of the rocks to form a bubbling pond. This massive spring widens and deepens as it carries onward downstream. Its source is the melting snow on nearby Mount Hermon, which supplies a rich aquifer able to sustain the spring's year-round flow. This water is a treasure in the parched Middle East.

Our question in this chapter, "Why read the Bible?" is answered by God's challenge to Israel in Jeremiah. God is offering himself to us as living water today, just as he did thousands of years ago to the citizens of Jerusalem. Jesus, as reported in John 4, presented himself as the source of living water to the woman at the well in Samaria. This water changed her life and the life of her village. Later, at the Temple in Jerusalem, Jesus stood up and announced to the crowds:

> *"If anyone is thirsty, let him come to me and drink.*
> *Whoever believes in me, as the Scripture has said,*
> *streams of living water will flow from within him."*
> *By this he meant the Spirit, whom those who*
> *believed in him were later to receive.*
>
> —John 7:37-38 NIV

The premise of the Bible, then, is that our souls are thirsty for God himself, and the Bible promises that God freely supplies what we thirst for. But our skepticism reigns. Thus many of us carve our private cisterns, creating parched souls while ignoring God's overflowing goodness.

A Matter of Priorities

"I've got *so* much to do in so little time; it's hard to know where to fit Bible reading into my schedule— although I *know* it's important!" This honest sentiment reminds us of how hard it is to grow spiritually. It also explains how the rock-chiseling audience of Jeremiah's Jerusalem neglected God. Once we've embarked on a lifestyle of carving cisterns, it's hard to change. The neglect of God and the Bible comes from being busy in a world filled with urgent activism.

The problem, though, is deeper than our being "busy." The issue dawned on me some years ago as I was corresponding with a girlfriend who lived in Seattle while I was attending seminary near Chicago. She was wonderfully faithful in writing at least once, and sometimes twice, each week. Then came an unexpected two-week dry spell during which I didn't receive any letters. Finally the drought ended when a warm letter arrived, which included an explanation of why she had been too busy to write.

A significant insight came out of that small episode. It occurred to me that when we say we're "too busy," it's actually a less direct (and less self-revealing) way of saying, "I had other priorities." That is, to say, "I'm busy" is to shift blame to a set of external forces—while suggesting that I really *wanted* to do otherwise. There's some validity in the claim, of course: the external forces may be our job or some other contractual commitment. But even a job can be rejected or a contract renegotiated if they violate our deepest values. In reality, we usually have substantial freedom to pursue our priorities. Thus, to speak about priorities, rather than busyness, is to reveal our personal values—that we've embraced one activity instead of other options because we value that activity more. Jesus pressed a Galilee audience toward this kind of honest assessment when he reminded them, "No one can serve two masters. Either he will hate the one and love the other, or he will be devoted to the one and despise the other" (Matthew 6:24 NIV).

Since that insight dawned on me, I've weighed my priorities with greater care. At the most profound level—taking this from Jeremiah—the angels in heaven may be wondering even today why our priorities don't include staying in much closer contact with God. After all, as Paul shares in Ephesians 2:10, we were created by God for good works he prepared beforehand for us to fulfill. He is our living water; he made us with a plan in mind; and he wants us to trust him in all of life's demands.

I'll tell a story later in the book about Sam, but a preview is in order here. Sam was a retired missionary who read through the Bible two to three times a year for over 50 years. I was astonished at his pace, comparing it to my chapter-a-day devotional routine. When I asked him how he had time for all that reading he leaned back and smiled, saying, "Well, we take time for what we think is important, don't we?"

With that as a nudge, we return to our question: Why read the Bible? We can enlarge the answer: Because God offers himself to us as living water, and Jesus, in John chapters 8 and 15, tells us that if we claim to belong to him we need to "abide" in his Word and to "abide" in his love. These calls by Christ are both relational and practical.

Later, in the chapter titled "Meeting the Author of the Bible," we'll learn more about the subjective dimension of knowing God. For now, in the balance of this chapter, we'll look at the question in somewhat more objective terms. What, for instance, did he have in mind when he created us? Why are we here?

Before we go on to answer those questions, I want to introduce you to Carrie. She illustrates how a sense of purpose—"hope"—can make a dramatic difference in the way we live. During my seminary years I worked part of the time at a hospital caring for patients who were struggling with spiritual, mental, emotional, and social disorders. Carrie stands out in my memory of those days. She was then a 16-year-old who had lost her mother, and then her best friend to violent deaths—murder and suicide. When her father remarried Carrie wasn't ready—she wanted Dad for herself. In the ensuing competition Carrie's father decided to make things easier on his new wife by sending Carrie to a boarding school. That felt like another death to Carrie. She became deeply depressed; there no longer seemed to be any point in living.

We received Carrie at the hospital after one of her many suicide attempts. Each attempt had been more serious than the last and our job, as she arrived at the hospital, was to help stabilize her and to stir enough courage in her to reengage life. By the time we received her she was so intent on taking her own life she had to be placed on 24-hour suicide prevention watch, where she stayed for weeks, not days, with no improvement. But let me defer the rest of Carrie's story until later in the chapter, after we've had a chance to think about God's purpose for creating us, his plan to communicate with us, and his willingness to put up with a fallen world—the kind of world that was so painful for Carrie.

Realizing Our Purpose in Life

God is greater than our best thoughts can fathom. Yet we still need to ask, "Why did God create us?" A good place to begin answering the question is in a catechism of the Westminster Assembly of the seventeenth century. "What," they asked, "is the chief end of man?" The right response is: "Man's chief end is to glorify God and to enjoy him forever." The call to glorify God is, indeed, firmly rooted in all of Scripture. First Corinthians 10:31, for instance, tells us, "So whether you eat or drink or whatever you do, do it all for the glory of God" (NIV).

Author John Piper recently put a slightly new spin on the old catechism by suggesting that the message of the better answer is that we should glorify God *by* enjoying him forever. The obvious point, of course, is that the relational aspect of God's creation is crucial. I agree. But I'm not satisfied that the Westminster tradition gets it right, even with Piper's modified emphasis.

The method, though, makes sense: We can assume that any command by God must tell us *something* about the point of our creation. Thus, the question about our "chief end" is linked to our original question: "Why read the Bible?" The Bible, after all, is something like an operator's manual, and we are the objects whose proper operations are being explained in it. If the chief end of man is to glorify God and to enjoy him, then that must be the chief purpose we were made for. But before agreeing with that assertion, we need to review what the Bible actually says about our ultimate purpose.

Perhaps the clearest answer is found in John 17. This chapter is remarkable because it offers the longest and most personal communication of the entire Bible between the Son and the Father. In it the Son opens his soul to the Father as he prays on behalf of his disciples. There we discover that God's purpose is to create a unity between the Father, the Son, and those whom the Father has given to the Son—those who believe in him. The motive for this is love. In this love a dynamic selflessness and mutual glorification is disclosed in the triune community of the Godhead. This existed even before the world was created. The language of glory in John 17 suffuses the prayer: "Father, the hour has come; glorify Thy Son, that the Son may glorify Thee" (verse 1). But we also discover that love and glory are companion concepts. That is, the nature of love is to glorify the one who is beloved.

I've seen this link between love and glory in my role as a professor. Over the years I've watched a host of relationships form and blossom to marriage. In each case the partners treated their beloved companion as the most profound discovery of life—and with that came the assumption that they were more blessed than any other person alive. More than once I've see a young woman who was considered "nice" suddenly magnified into someone "wonderful" by the gushing young man who had come to treasure her. That, my friends, is glory! And mutual glorification is what wedding services are all about.

It is this mutuality of glory, based on love, that we find between the Son and the Father in John 17: Glorify me, so I can glorify you. Jesus prayed, "I have brought you glory on earth by completing the work you gave me to do. And now, Father, glorify me in your presence with the glory I had with you before the world began" (John 17:4-5 NIV). One aspect of glory came from Jesus' response to his Father's mission for him. This was expressed earlier in the gospel when Jesus announced, "The hour has come for the Son of Man to be glorified" when a group of Greeks sought to speak with him (John 12:23). That encounter marked a shift in the gospel from Christ's public ministry to his passion— the week that led to his crucifixion and burial. Jesus responded to the Greek request by explaining, "[When] I am lifted up from the earth"—a euphemism for his crucifixion—"[I] will draw all men to Myself" (John 12:32). That is, he would make himself accessible to all mankind (including the Greeks) by his crucifixion. The key to this new accessibility was his willingness to die. Death and glory were one and the same.

But we must not miss what stands behind the mutual glorification of the Son and the Father. It was motivated by love: "Father, I want those you have given me to be with me where I am, and to see my glory, the glory you have given me *because you loved me* before the creation of the world" (John 17:24 NIV, emphasis added). Christ's death solved our problem of sin and opened the door for us to see and experience his glory.

Thus we discover that the love of God has been the chief quality of the Trinitarian communion from before the world was created. It continues after the problem of sin is confronted so we can join God's fellowship of love and glory for the rest of eternity. John, then, can say truly, "God is love" (1 John 4:8).

What, then, is our creation purpose? The Bible tells us we were designed to be lovers—created in the image of God, who is Love. Genuine disciples are characterized by their love for each other (John 13:35) because we have been united with the glorious love of God through regeneration:

> *I have given them the glory that you gave me, that they may be one as we are one: I in them and you in me. May they be brought to complete unity to let the world know that you sent me and have loved them even as you have loved me....I have made you known to them, and will continue to make you known in order that the love you have for me may be in them and that I myself may be in them.*
> —John 17:22-23,26 NIV

It is no surprise, then, that when Jesus was asked the New Testament-era equivalent of the question, "What is the chief end of man?"—which then was framed as, "What is the greatest commandment for us to live by?"—he answered by quoting Deuteronomy 6:4-5.

> *"The most important one," answered Jesus, "is this: 'Hear, O Israel, the Lord our God, the Lord is one. Love the Lord your God with all your heart and with all your soul and with all your mind and with all your strength.'"*
>
> —Mark 12:29-30 NIV

How does the call for glory relate to love, then? As a fruit, not a duty. We delight to glorify the one we love.

There is a serious danger, by the way, in replacing love with glory as man's chief end. It places the behavior—giving glory—above the motive behind it—loving God. Because a behavior doesn't always display the underlying motive, we can be captured by hypocrisy—the error of the Pharisees—by pretending to glorify God without loving him.

The great biblical example of giving glory without love is found in the book of Esther. There we find the Jewish protagonist, Mordecai, is despised by the antagonist, Haman. In an ironic reversal Haman is forced to glorify Mordecai—despite still hating him—with the same glory Haman wanted for himself. A crucial principle is illustrated by the story: The relationship between love and glory can only be certified in a single direction. Love *always* expresses itself by giving glory; but glory can be given *without* being motivated by love. Thus, love is prior to glory as man's chief end—and love, once awakened, will always seek to glorify God.

To love God, then, is what we were made for, and the Bible is God's love letter to us—an invitation to abide in his love by abiding in his Word. As one of the early English Puritans, Richard Sibbes, put it, God created us "because he has a spreading goodness." We come to the Bible because in it we are able to "taste and see that the LORD is good"! (Psalm 34:8).

The Bible, God's Letter to Us

The Bible, viewed as God's love letter to his beloved children, assumes that God is a willing and able communicator. The Bible is his direct line to humanity, the place where he tells us about himself. He uses it to speak to our minds and hearts, to nourish our souls. He offers us hope, expresses his love, and commands our respect. Why read the Bible? Because it serves to interpret all that we experience in life in light of God's love and greatness.

Not everyone, of course, is ready to share that assumption, but the Bible invites us to embrace it as the starting point. The Bible, for instance, begins without a preamble as it informs us in Genesis 1:1, "In the beginning God created the heavens and the earth." There you have it—whether we accept it or deny it, the Bible goes on from there to tell us God's point of view about things. In the New Testament the Gospel of John intentionally adopts the same refrain in its first verse: "In the beginning was the Word...." So rather than debate the question of whether the Bible is God's only Word, his inerrant Word, or just a product of human reflections, we will assume that God is a good communicator when he chooses to speak. His use of fallible human agents—the Bible writers—isn't an obstacle to an all-powerful God.

The fact that the Bible is actually a collection of writings gathered from a number of locations and periods of history makes this whole question of God's revelation a complex matter. The study of these questions is called

"Bible Introduction." For those who are ready to pursue such matters be sure to look at the section, "Resources for Bible Reading" on page 157. I've found matters of Bible Introduction fascinating, stretching, and reassuring.

The Bible's Claims About God's Communication

God may be a good communicator, but why do we need the Bible to hear from him? Does the Bible even claim to be God's self-disclosure to humanity? If so, what does it say about his intentions? In asking these questions while reading through the Bible we discover that God's plan to communicate with us through the Bible is presented as its very fabric. Throughout the Scriptures we find assertions that God "spoke" or "appeared" to his prophets. "Hear the Word of the Lord" is a refrain that echoes throughout the Old Testament. God warned the people of Israel, after they agreed to be his priestly nation (in Exodus 19–24), that they were obliged to keep the laws that he "commanded" them to obey. Indeed, the whole point of their role as a priestly nation was to share with other nations and to model what they heard from God.

God ensured that the communication was reliable. He instructed the prophet Jeremiah, for instance, to warn deceptive prophets—those who claimed to be receiving dreams from God when, in actuality, they made them up. God would have none of this. It was like comparing wheat with chaff. God's Word, he declared to Jeremiah, is "like fire" and "like a hammer which shatters a rock" (Jeremiah 23:29).

The Bible also states and restates that God means to guide us—something appropriate to what it means for him to be God. He holds us accountable if we fail to respond. He always proclaims his warnings before handing out any punishments. The Israelites, for instance, were warned early and often that they were, as God's people, to be holy.

Moses, in Deuteronomy, reminded them, "If you are not careful to observe all the words of this law which are written in this book, to fear this honored and awesome name, the LORD your God, then the LORD will bring extraordinary plagues on you" (Deuteronomy 28:58-59). Similarly, God spoke through Jeremiah to warn the Chaldeans, saying, "I will bring upon that land all My words which I have pronounced against it, all that is written in this book, which Jeremiah has prophesied against all the nations" (Jeremiah 25:13).

In the New Testament we find that God's biblical guidance equips us for successful living. Consider Paul's reminder to his student Timothy:

> . . . *how from infancy you have known the holy Scriptures, which are able to make you wise for salvation through faith in Christ Jesus. All Scripture is God-breathed and is useful for teaching, rebuking, correcting and training in righteousness, so that the man of God may be thoroughly equipped for every good work.*
>
> —2 Timothy 3:15-16 NIV

In the book of Revelation we also find a New Testament warning just as compelling as the Old Testament warning proclaimed by Moses:

> *I warn everyone who hears the words of the prophecy of this book: If anyone adds anything to them, God will add to him the plagues described in this book. And if anyone takes words away from this book of prophecy, God will take away from him his share in the tree of life and in the holy city, which are described in this book.*
>
> —Revelation 22:18-19 NIV

The Bible, then, includes very direct statements about God's intention to speak to us, and about the importance of reading what he sent us through his inspired writers. The content of the Bible is well-woven with such themes. Yet the Bible is more than a set of propositions meant to inform about God and to correct our misapprehensions. If examined from a certain distance, we discover an overall shape that stands out among the particular elements. A fad that attracted a lot of attention a few years ago offers a partial analogy for this. Viewers would be invited to stare at an apparently meaningless field of spots generated by a computer and printed on a poster. After gazing for some time, the viewer would finally find the correct focal distance and discover in the poster a three-dimensional form. So it is that the Bible reader begins to see in the Bible (though it is much more overt than the computer pictures) the looming presence of Christ in both the Old and New Testaments.

The Importance of Christ in God's Communication

Christ is the object of faith and the focal center of biblical revelation. Trusting his Word is the cure to sin: "If you abide in my word," Jesus told some erstwhile believers, "then you are truly disciples of Mine; and you shall know the truth, and the truth shall make you free" (John 8:31-32). Free from what? Jesus answered: a freedom from sin.

The importance of Christ Jesus in God's self-disclosure cannot be overstated. He is the anticipated Messiah in the Old Testament and the crucified Savior and Son of God in the New Testament. The function of God's communication to the world has Christ at its center. A book by John W. Wenham, *Christ and the Bible*, summarizes the case very effectively. Belief in the authority of the Bible, he points out, comes as the fruit of a faith in Christ rather than vice versa. Jesus affirmed the reliability of the Old Testament—it serves as a direct testimony to his person and work—and he assured his disciples that the Spirit would superintend their accurate recall of his ministry—the foundation of the New Testament. Thus, for the person who receives Christ as Lord, it is incumbent on that person to adopt his Lord's point of view about the Scriptures.

This certainty that God has communicated with us in Christ is rooted in the resurrection of Jesus, an event that is historically certain just as it is reported in the New Testament—and, it should be noted, also reflected in other ancient sources. Paul, in 1 Corinthians 15:12-19, goes so far as to acknowledge that Christianity is empty of significance without the resurrection of Jesus: "If Christ has not been raised, then our preaching is vain, your faith also is vain" (verse 14). The resurrection validates Christ's claims, displaying his power over death and his ability to solve the problem of sin and death on our behalf.

God, then, wants humanity to know him, his ways, his will, and the Son he sent to save us. The Bible reflects a consistent awareness of the battle between those opposed to God and those captured by God's love and truth. The battle is ultimately one of trust: Either we embrace God and his trustworthiness, or we trust the assumptions offered by one who has promoted a radical skepticism about God and his Word from the time of the Garden of Eden until now.

God's Communication and the Problem of Sin

A very sophisticated theologian was once asked to summarize his theology. He responded by repeating the Sunday-school chorus: "Jesus loves me, this I know, for the Bible tells me so." Simple yet true. God cares for his proud, skeptical, and needy world in a manner that should astonish us, given the sinful animosity the world has shown him throughout history. Jesus summarized this love for a guest, a teacher named Nicodemus, one evening: "For God so loved the world the he gave his one and only Son, that whoever believes in him shall not perish but have eternal life" (John 3:16 NIV). Rather than allowing his chosen ones to die eternally, Jesus suffered death on our behalf.

Where did the problem of sin first emerge? And what is the nature of that problem? In opening chapters of the Bible, we see sin on display. It was a battle of conflicting promises: Satan, the serpent, pitted his word against God's word. God had warned Adam not to eat from the tree of the knowledge of good and evil "for in the day you eat from it you shall surely die" (Genesis 2:17). The serpent denied God's word, saying, "You surely shall not die!" (Genesis 3:4).

It's fair to say that the rest of the Bible is an extension of this debate. God offers his truth; the devil offers his lies. Who will be believed? The question is fundamental, so much so that believing God's Word is the chief function of faith. It reflects the cure to the lie first offered in the Garden of Eden: "Faith," Paul tells us, "comes from hearing, and hearing by the word of Christ" (Romans 10:17).

It is precisely the exercise of faith-building through God's Word that is the "plot line" of most Bible narratives. Rather than merely offering a collection of stories, the Bible chronicles the ongoing battle between sinful skepticism and godly faith. Scripture traces the tension of faith versus unfaith again and again, whether in the stories of individuals such as Abraham and Jacob, or in groups such as Israel and Judah.

In 1 Kings 17, for instance, the prophet Elijah met a widow who was preparing a final meal for herself and her son. A famine had ruined them and their food was gone. Elijah requested that she feed *him* her last meal—a dramatic test of her faith. The prophet assured her that

Yahweh would supply all her needs, so that her basic supplies of flour and oil would not be exhausted. She gave Elijah the meal and the promise was fulfilled, "according to the word of the LORD which He spoke through Elijah" (1 Kings 17:16).

In the next chapter, 1 Kings 18, we find the story of the competition between Elijah and the prophets of Baal on Mount Carmel. Once again the polarity of faith and unfaith is central—forcing a decision on whether Yahweh or Baal is truly God. Elijah was outnumbered by overwhelming odds: 450 priests of Baal to one for Yahweh. Ahab, moved by his foreign wife, Jezebel, had supported the worship of Baal and suppressed the worship of Yahweh. The test of which God was the true God centered on the ability of the opposed deities: Could Baal, the storm-god, produce fire from heaven to devour a sacrifice? If he couldn't, Yahweh would.

Elijah waited on the prophets of Baal as they attempted to stir their god to action. Elijah, although standing alone amid a hostile crowd, mocked the priests as they carried out their rituals. The event ended when Elijah, having soaked his altar in water, prayed, "O LORD, God of Abraham, Isaac and Israel, let it be known today that you are God in Israel and that I am your servant and have done all these things *at your command*" (1 Kings 18:36 NIV, emphasis added). Yahweh, of course, devoured the entire altar—animal, wood, water, and stone—by fire from heaven in support of the word he had given through Elijah.

The point of the vast number of true "faith stories" in the Bible is to reinforce the faith of individual readers, even when we feel like the king is opposed to us and the number of unbelievers around us is running at the same ratio Elijah experienced among the prophets of Baal. The Spirit of God takes the Word of God and produces faith in God as we read.

Skepticism toward God is the product of sin in the modern world, just as it was in the ancient days of the Bible. It may be even harder today because we don't have any prophets like Elijah among us to produce such dramatic public miracles. The pressures to bow to the cultural values around us can be intense. The reality, however, is that Yahweh is God, and his values work while others fail.

What God and His Word Can Do

It's time to return to my encounter with Carrie. She had tasted the fruit of a world without God and was now hopeless. I asked her whether she looked forward to anything in life—whether she had any hope at all. She didn't like the question because it was painful: "If I try to look ahead all I see is blackness. There's no light at all."

"If I were able to bring someone to meet with you who has gone through some of the same kinds of tragedy you've experienced, but who has come out the other side—would that be helpful to you?" I asked.

She looked up from the floor for the first time, her eyes wide. "Could you do that? I really need to talk to someone who knows what this feels like!"

"No, Carrie, I'm afraid we don't have anyone like that." I paused. "But you can be that person for someone else in the days to come. However, you need to be willing to find hope for yourself first…and then you can share it with others. Are you willing to become that person, ready to help someone like yourself in another year or two?"

I'm not sure what she thought, but I suspect there was a conflict between a glimpse of light in her darkness and the fear that she might be crushed again if she reopened her soul to hope.

"But, I don't know how to find hope."

"My question is whether you're willing to look for it. All of us live with some sort of hope, and I'm sure you can find hope for yourself, but you have to be open to it."

She was quiet for some moments.

"I'm willing to try."

I asked her whether she could think of sources of hope. She suggested that religion seemed to help some people. I asked whether it was religion, or God, that made the difference.

"It has to be God."

"So how do we get in touch with God?" I asked. "Where does he offer any hope to us?"

I'm sure some of the staff attached to our unit would not have voted for the line I was taking with Carrie, but nothing else had worked during her many weeks with us.

"In the Bible, I suppose."

Thankfully our hospital had a Christian heritage, and spiritual support was part of the philosophy of patient care for those who were open to it. The approach I was taking with Carrie occurred to me during my personal Bible reading that morning. I cared for Carrie but, like the rest of the staff, didn't know where to begin with her. Losing her mother and her best friend had been traumatic—and the evil behind her losses was very real and terribly painful. During my Bible reading, Carrie had come to mind when I read 2 Corinthians 1:3-4:

> *Praise be to the God and Father of our Lord Jesus Christ, the Father of compassion and the God of all comfort, who comforts us in all our troubles, so that we can comfort those in any trouble with the comfort we ourselves have received from God (NIV).*

It jumped out at me that Carrie's pain could actually become a platform for helping others like herself, but only if she were willing to let God into her life to comfort her. I broached the idea to her as we read this passage together from a Bible in the unit library.

"Would you be willing to let God comfort you? I suspect you're pretty angry at God right now—as much as you believe in him—so you'll have to quit waving your fist in his face for this to happen."

We talked at some length, and she agreed to memorize the verses as a starting point. A few days later one of the Christian nurses in the unit told me that Carrie had expressed her personal faith in Christ—the fist was starting to open, to becoming an open hand now ready to receive comfort.

About three years later I heard from Carrie as she was doing some volunteer work with some troubled young women. "You can say, 'I told you so!'" she wrote. The 2 Corinthian verses were now true in her experience as she discovered unusual success in helping these women. Since then I've continued to hear from Carrie on holidays, and was delighted with the news of her marriage, a son, and a doctorate in psychology in the years that followed. Here was a woman who had tasted the living water offered by God. It refreshed her soul, and she now offers her hope to others.

3

The Transforming Impact of the Bible

Have you ever had a conversation with Jesus? I have. I'd like to share what I've learned from him. Let me say right away, though, that I haven't had visions or heard voices—nothing of that sort! Yet I have conversations with him just as certainly as I have conversations with my family and friends. Jesus is alive—he continues to speak and act on a daily basis. And my interaction with him is not unique, but is available to everyone. We discover, just as his Galilean apostles did, that he alone has the words of life—that he responds to our questions and draws us into a transforming faith. He moves us from darkness to light, from empty activism to an active peace, from a love of self to a love of God.

How and where does Jesus speak so clearly and effectively? In the Bible. When does he speak to me? When I read the Bible. What makes me so certain God speaks by the Bible? Because, as we've seen already, the Bible regularly claims to be the Word of God. The claim is affirmed by Jesus, whose credibility is established by his resurrection. Furthermore, the Word is alive. God answers my questions about life in the Bible; and his answers force me to ask new questions that he then answers. It's a conversation that never ends as long as I keep asking my questions and reading my Bible. Scripture is where I first heard his voice, speaking to my questions as effectively as my father did when I was a child. The Bible, I found, is the Word of God, which the Spirit of God uses to speak to the children of God. I've come to be assured that the Bible is God's objective, propositional, and historical Word *before* I encounter it. Yet it also *becomes* the words of God *for me* as I engage it, by the Spirit, in the activities of life. These are the foundations of a living faith. Indeed, we're all called by Jesus to abide in him—in his love and his Word (John 15:1-11).

For centuries the Spirit has worked through the Bible to unleash his transforming love in human lives. Martin Luther was captured by Paul's statement in Romans that "the just shall live by faith." As Luther and the other early reformers grasped that truth and shared it with others, Europe was turned upside down. The Puritans in England and America were men and women willing to face exile from the comforts of home and friends for the sake of preaching the Word. The French Huguenots were people of the Word even amid some harsh persecutions. The great missionary efforts of Christianity have all been initiated by Christians whose lives were profoundly shaped by the Word.

Look into history for any Christian whose life and ministry has made a lasting mark, and at the heart of that ministry is the message of the Word, revealing Christ, embedded in the living flesh and blood of their human activities. Richard Sibbes spoke of this ministry and its main focus, Christ:

Among many others, this is one main end—"to lay open the unsearchable riches of Christ." Therein you have something of Christ unfolded, of his natures, offices, and benefits we have by him—redemption, and freedom, and a right to all things in him, the excellencies of another world.

—Works of Richard Sibbes, 2.184

Young Christians who are ready to grow—"longing for the pure milk of the word"—need to discover the Bible as God's primary tool for discipleship. We need full portions—first the milk, then the meat—to be transformed in today's challenging world!

My Story

I was raised in an evangelical Christian family. That was a problem because it tended to be a veil, a very comfortable veil, that blocked my ability to see my real condition. I was so certain that I was already a Christian—a certainty rooted in some childhood expressions of faith—that it didn't seem necessary to revisit the issues of faith at a basic level. I wasn't asking hard questions about God, life, and faith.

The process of my conversion to a living faith in Christ was initially stimulated by the death of a high-school classmate. Dave Goff of Glasgow, Montana, died in a motorcycle accident during the winter of my sophomore year. At 15 I hadn't been that close to death before. A grandparent's death, yes, but never a peer. The Friday night after he died I went to a friend's home, along with a number of others, for what I thought would be shared commiseration. Not so—it was simply a weekend party, with music, dancing, punch, and light chatter. Dave was hardly mentioned in the 30 minutes I was there. As I left Tom Bussing was just ahead of me, leaving as well.

"Where are *you* going?" I asked.

"Home—this just isn't for me, not with Dave gone."

The two of us found a place to talk. Why did Dave have to die so young? Or more to the point, why had Dave ever lived? What meaning does life carry if someone is so easily forgotten? What of Tom and myself—if either of us died, would we be forgotten just as quickly? What if we became more "significant," important enough to be famous figures in history? Each of us paused, thinking about how little excitement our high school history courses raised. So much for fame! Fortune wasn't particularly intriguing either—at least not when it was set next to death. You work for wealth all your life and then die. It didn't seem like an enticing prospect. We wrestled with the issues for an hour, maybe two, and eventually concluded that meaning or significance had to come from someone greater than ourselves. Was God the answer? He might be, but neither of us was sure that our family Gods—his Catholic and mine Baptist—added much to the conversation that evening. Indeed, I wondered, *Is God really "there"?*

The unsettled question of God and meaning stayed with me in the months that followed. My father retired from the Air Force that summer and hoped to fly commercially. Using two cars, we drove from Montana through Seattle, Los Angeles, Salt Lake City, Denver, Rapid City, and once again, Montana. An unseen hand was at work in the itinerary, preparing me for my first real conversation with Christ. Younger brother Dave was in the Volkswagen for a rare shift and I was napping in the Pontiac when mother mentioned Big Timber. We had already made a U-turn in Billings an hour earlier in order to take the scenic route through Bozeman. "The church camp you sent me to last year," I mentioned in passing, "is just 35 miles south of here, down that gravel road." "Oh...why don't we go there for a visit?" she suggested. I gave a startled "Sure!" On arriving we discovered that two members of the boys' work crew had broken their summer contract and were leaving camp the next day. Bill and I were recruited on the spot as replacements.

When the high-school campers arrived, those of us on the staff were assimilated among the regular campers. Against all odds (I was young and quiet) I was elected by the other campers to be a president, one of three among the 100 or so campers. The position called for me to be a spiritual leader among my peers. Spiritual leader! I wasn't even sure God existed, but I was now starting to doubt my own skepticism—could it be that God was at work here? The campers had an extended break in the program soon after the election and I took it as a chance to confront God—assuming he had a hand in shaping my circumstances—and left the camp for a hillside just to the east, Bible in hand. I came back two hours later, having met God in a life-changing encounter.

A Startling Realization

My conversion, more than anything else, was a discovery—a surprised realization that I was loved. The event itself was an encounter with a real person, with someone I'd never met before although I knew something about him. Jesus turned out to be a much stronger personality than my Sunday-school training led me to expect.

"Okay, God," I said to the empty space around me, "if you're out here, I need to hear from you! Whatever and however, I've *got* to hear from you. To be very honest, I'm not sure that you *really* exist, and whether it's *you* who got me back here to Clydehurst. And if you're doing all this, why? Am I your puppet? Do you want something from me?"

Maybe, I reflected, *this is all just a coincidence.* A soft breeze stirred the grassy slope.

"God, I've heard that you can speak through burning bushes—there are lots of bushes around here; or just speak out of heaven—you're God, you can do whatever you want! So here I am, ready to listen." Birds chattered in the surrounding pines.

"Okay, God, it might be that you won't speak to me because I'm just curious rather than serious." What might convince him?

"Whatever you want! If you have something that you want from me, just let me know." I paused before offering my ultimate concession.

"I'll even be a missionary if that's what it takes."

Serene clouds made ever-changing backdrops to the impassive mountains across the valley floor, while the Boulder River sparkled under the early afternoon sun. Wildflowers on the slope below me startled the brown and green forest hues with vivid flecks of color. An hour came and left. If God wouldn't be rushed, I would wait.

Other reflections stirred through my mind. If God existed, but somehow had no voice, what could we do but go on without him? If he *wouldn't* speak—after I'd made my unconditioned vow—then what else could be done except to go on without him? Or if he only speaks to some, and not to others, all I could do is say, "God, I'm here too!" and hope for the best.

In my musing a new presence broke in, an inaudible but distinct counterpoint to my growing impatience with the silent God. Why not, it occurred to me, read the Bible? Or, to be honest, the thought was closer to "Why, *dummy*, don't you read your Bible if you're so anxious to hear from God?!"

I happened to have my Bible with me. In fact, I was sitting on it. I knew, of course, that the Bible was regularly tagged as "the Word of God," but I also knew that childhood memorization efforts and Sunday-school classes led to a familiarity that produced a yawning indifference. Jesus, usually carrying little lambs and wearing what to my small mind looked like colorless Hawaiian muumuus, held little fascination for me. As I grew up I learned I needed salvation. Not much else registered with me, least of all reading the Bible just to read the Bible. I also knew that the Bible wasn't alone in claiming to be God's Word. Still, I was determined to explore any option in order to hear from God, so I picked up the Bible.

I started in the first book of the New Testament, Matthew. It began, of course, with flannelgraph familiarity: the story of the nativity, then the baptism and temptation of Jesus, followed by the calling of his disciples. It was in the Sermon on the Mount that Jesus stepped out of the glowing "head of Christ" image I grew up with into the flinty but caring controversialist he's been to me ever since. When he talked about lust and suggested that a plucked-out eye is a better option than the judgment, or that a chopped-off hand is better than continued use of that hand in sin, I recognized the hyperbole but I also caught the urgency of his point. Jesus wasn't speaking in the half-measures of a socialized spirituality but of radical surgery of the soul. My own teenage appetites, although largely unfed, were already charting a course that Jesus, who was now disclosing himself to me in the Bible, clearly anticipated.

"No one," Jesus warned, "can serve two masters; for either he will hate the one and love the other, or he will hold to one and despise the other! You cannot serve God and mammon" (Matthew 6:24). His finger was pointed at the center of my soul. It dawned on me that until now I actually had a domesticated God, one who would serve me as I offered him some modest devotion. My teenage version of a divine-human reciprocity treaty envisioned a God who could be placated with just enough attention to then overlook the small vices that give life its best flavors. But now I was faced with the unyielding gaze of Jesus, who spoke in terms of "love" and "hate"—the language of unbalanced passions rather than of practical equilibrium. How, then, I thought in response, does a man make a career if it isn't through devotion to his human masters? Isn't money the sign of success? And isn't a successful career a noble goal?

Jesus answered, "Look at the birds of the air...Observe how the lilies of the field grow...even Solomon in all his glory did not clothe himself like one of these" (Matthew 6:26,28-29). The beauty of my Montana setting scored the point for God. "Will He not much more do so for you, O men of little faith?" (verse 30).

By now I was well into the conversation. "So what do you want of me, Lord?"

He answered, "Seek *first* his kingdom and his righteousness and let *him* be concerned with your affairs and needs in life."

In that moment it struck me: The meaning in life that Tom and I wondered about *was* found in God! His care for me was greater than my own self-care; and by caring first for him I gave myself over to Meaning himself, and could rest in the certainty that whatever he made me for would, indeed, be accomplished not by duty-driven efforts but by an honest response to him. My tour of the western United States, whatever its impact on the others in my family, was for me God's loving pursuit of an unworthy teenager.

I responded. "O Lord, here I am. I *do* want you as my God and master." Meaning had come from the One with whom I was now speaking, not from anything I might ever do. God loved me. That was enough. Yet my first instinct was to share my discovery. While the moment wasn't one of ecstasy or euphoria—rather, a peace with a profound sense of worth—I knew that I had met with God himself and now belonged to him.

God Speaks in the Bible

The foundation laid for the rest of life, based on my Montana encounter, was that God is living, active, and speaks clearly through the Bible. My deepest questions were met there. The first moments of my new faith supported the lesson. I continued to read. *Lord,* I thought, *where do I go from here? How does it work in practice to make you first in life?* A moment later I read, "Ask, and it shall be given to you; seek, and you shall find; knock, and it shall be opened to you. For everyone who asks receives, and he who seeks finds, and to him who knocks it shall be opened" (Matthew 7:7).

This was so simple, yet I hadn't grasped it despite being raised in a Christian home and in Bible-centered churches. Was this something that only certain people understood? He responded, "Enter by the narrow gate; for the gate is wide, and the way is broad that leads to destruction, and many are those who enter by it. For the gate is small, and the way is narrow that leads to life, and few are those who find it" (7:13-14).

Lord, does that mean that not everyone in the church is necessarily a real believer?

"On the day of judgment many will say to me, 'Lord, Lord, didn't we prophesy, cast out demons, and perform lots of miracles in your name?' Then I'll tell them, 'I never even knew you; leave me, then, you who lived in your independence!'" (see Matthew 7:22-23).

As I read onward I asked myself, is it *really* possible that God is caring for me in such personal terms, or is this my imagination? Soon I came to his reassuring response, "Aren't two sparrows sold for a penny? Yet none of them ever falls to the ground without your Father's care; as for you, even the hairs on your head are numbered. Rest assured, you're much more important than the sparrows!" (see Matthew 10:30-31). With that, I left the sparrows of my Montana hillside and went back to the camp with a transformed heart. God himself had spoken to me.

The Legacy of Art, Sam, and Jack

Art

After our time at Clydehurst, Bill and I rejoined the family, now settled in Spokane. Our new church offered an awkward high school youth program as they tried to come to grips with how to use their first-ever youth pastor. The Sunday school was still under a Christian Education director, while our Sunday evening activity, Christian Endeavor, was led separately by some volunteers. Art, the relatively new youth pastor, was given the leftover time to work with us. As I remember it, the Sunday school had between 120 to 150 participants, the evening program averaged 35, and Art was only able to recruit about 20 of us for his activities. Despite his small piece of the pie, it was Art who made all the difference. His threefold ministry strategy featured use of the summer church camp, a midweek study of basic theology (four or five of us came regularly), and separate home Bible studies for each of the city high schools.

Art was robust in everything he did. In water skiing he overmatched all of us who thought we had something to brag about. At the summer camp Art would take any three of us with him when it was time to toss him in the river. He could also hike our legs off—a man's man who commanded respect and affection. His hallmark, whether he ever realized it or not, was a regular refrain, "Oh you guys, taste and see, the Lord is good!" However pious and saccharine that might sound in some people, it was as natural in Art as green is to grass. Most of all he was devoted to us with the kind of individual care that I still find rare among church leaders. For example, my Montana conversion hadn't changed my pre-conversion devotion to playing football. Art came to all of Shadle Park's games. Much more importantly he sometimes came to watch us practice, but he never made a production of it. Only two of us on the team attended the church.

After one practice he came alongside me and said, "Hey, Ron, why don't you come out to our Shadle Park Bible study? We'd love to have you!" The study met on Tuesday nights in a home near the school. I was hesitant. It was another night out and I wasn't sure what it had to offer. While I was avid to grow, hard experience had already set me back a bit. Sunday school, for instance, was an exercise of grinding through tedious booklets, led by Ben, our kind but uninspired teacher. The experience regularly reminded me of the visit I had with my cabin counselor at Clydehurst as I came back from the hillside.

"Carl," I said, "I finally figured out what it means to be a Christian! I gave myself completely to God."

"Well," he responded, "don't get *too* excited—these things come and go."

"No, no," I said, "this wasn't just some emotional thing; it came from what I was reading in Matthew. Jesus made it absolutely clear that he wanted my whole life and I gave it to him!"

"Okay, Ron, but just remember that after it subsides you don't need to feel guilty." I wondered why Carl and Ben weren't captured by God *himself* speaking to us in the Bible—wasn't this something to be excited about?

At my first Bible study with Art, in Sonny's home, the six of us sat around the dinner table. We just read from the Bible in sequential sections while Art explained the context and offered some comments along the way. He was taking us through the Old Testament, looking at the patriarchs, the judges, the kings and prophets; later we walked through the New Testament as well. A whole new world unfolded for me as an appetite for the Word, developed at Clydehurst, was now being fed. We saw how the promise God made in Eden—that the seed of the woman would crush the head of the serpent—was finally met in Jesus. Nations and individuals rebelled against God's rule, yet God always had his way. God's goodness came again and again to the humble, while the proud and strong were ultimately dismissed as fools in light of the upside-down values of the Bible. Jesus, although God in the flesh, was despised by his own religious community and crucified. Yet in his death he offered us life. At the end of our hour of study Art paused, "Let's take some time in prayer now. I hope you don't mind if I kneel." Most of us did the same. I found that the directness in prayer, a sense of our speaking to a real person, was as alive in Sonny's dining room as it had been for me on the Montana mountainside. I was home at last with a man who also knew the God who had captured my own heart.

Sam

Sam, the retired missionary I mentioned earlier, was planting a church in Sechelt on the coast of British Columbia north of Vancouver, and two of us on a summer mission were helping with the building construction. I had just graduated from high school and was ready to take on some new challenges. Indeed, the summer was to become a transition from Art's spiritual care to the self-feeding regime of adulthood.

We ate breakfast with Sam and his wife each morning at their beachside cottage before starting work. As something of a saintly gabber he was able to turn almost any subject into a Bible discourse. Trees, for instance. Did we know how important trees are in the Bible? From the tree of the knowledge of good and evil, to the branch of Judah, and finally to the tree that became the cross at Calvary, trees are crucial to the stories of the Bible. The tree of life, he pointed out, served as bookends to the Bible, being placed out of bounds for Adam and Eve in Genesis and then being restored to the saints in Revelation. The next morning he launched into the importance of Melchizedek, including his significance in Genesis, his office in Psalm 110, and the implications of both for Christ in the book of Hebrews.

What fascinated me was his offhanded access to the entire Bible—any section, whenever I raised a question, could be engaged with easy familiarity. It was functional knowledge, too. That is, he honored the context in making his points, he noticed the relation of a particular text to broader biblical themes, and he saw implications for present life. Yet his formal Bible training had been modest.

"Sam," I asked, "how did you learn to fit things together like you do? Did you take a Bible survey course somewhere?" He laughed. "I just read my Bible."

"How *much* reading—how do you approach it?"

"Oh, I suppose I get through it at least two or three times a year."

I almost spilled my coffee. "And how long have you been doing that?"

"Since I became a Christian. That was about 50 years ago."

"Do you mean to say that you've read through the entire Bible between 100 and 150 times?!"

"Well, I suppose that's right, now that you ask." His wife nodded in agreement.

"But how do you have the time?"

He looked a little surprised. "We make time for what's important to us, don't we? I just take time throughout the day, the way lots of people read novels or watch TV. My mornings are most important, but I also take some time at lunch and at night. Some afternoons I'll just read for two or three hours. It's food for my soul."

The challenge captured me. Each day as we finished work, or on the many days when we couldn't work, I went to a shaded spot on the pebbly beach—sometimes leaning back against my log to watch the eagles dive for salmon—and began my own reading.

Within two months I completed my first read-through. I was left in awe of God's greatness, holiness, and redemptive love. I saw the vast and singular strength of his personality projecting through the broad range of writers and circumstances in both testaments. I realized that God's personality is well defined in the Bible, offering me as real a relationship as any I might have with someone standing before me. The Clydehurst conversation was, indeed, just the beginning. Art helped by offering the historical framework for my reading and Sam gave me a model that eclipsed the very modest devotional approaches to the Bible that I had used before. So I began walking in Sam's footsteps during that magnificent summer, and to this day I still find each new read-through as productive as ever.

Jack

John G. Mitchell—or Jack—was a boilermaker from the north of England who emigrated to the plains of Canada and then to the States. In 1938 he and some others founded Multnomah School of the Bible—where I enrolled after my summer in Canada. Dr. Mitchell was a daunting figure in the classroom, forever challenging the collective students to fight him—with a grin—because of our pretended antagonism (*his* pretense, not ours!) to various biblical imperatives as they came up in his teaching. A sample of this was eventually posted on a plaque in the college library: "Don't you folks ever read your Bibles?!" I wonder, though, whether that quote really captured the man's heart. As often as not, his challenges about our Bible reading were soon afterwards followed with a much more serious note lilting through his Scots-like brogue. "Oh class, would that ye'd fall in love with the Savior." For Jack the two—Bible reading and a love for Christ—were a single fabric. To know Christ, we needed to know his Word. Not in part but in whole.

His example reinforced Sam's impact on me. Dr. Mitchell knew the Bible better than anyone in my experience and invited all of us to take Bible reading far more seriously than most Christians do. If a question was raised in class, whether related to the Bible text at hand or another, Mitchell would answer and then buttress his answer with an extended citation of Scripture. These quotes were usually at least a paragraph long. He'd say, as he looked toward the ceiling, "Now, that's in Hebrews 9, on the right side of the page, near the top. Check on me, but I think it says..." and he would go on to cite the passage flawlessly and at length. One day I asked him about it.

"Dr. Mitchell, how do you approach scripture memory? Do you have a special system?"

He smiled. "No, I just read it and read it; after a time it becomes familiar."

Some of his stories painted a more dynamic picture. As a young man in Canada, and just converted, he found the other men in his shop regularly challenging his new-found faith with their hardest questions. Mitchell, with only his Bible at hand, would go home and read until he found an answer for the next day. On some nights he got very little sleep. He soon began serving as a volunteer preacher among small churches in the plains provinces. His preparation was to read and reread his Bible segment until he knew it thoroughly. His lifelong habit of extensive Bible reading was well formed even before he went on to formal theological studies. Later his presence at Multnomah helped account for a core curriculum that requires more Bible and theology than any other Bible college I'm aware of—it properly generated the slogan, "If it's Bible you want, then you want Multnomah!"

Shattering the Boundaries

In reflecting on the lessons I gained from Art, Sam, and Jack, the greatest benefit wasn't so much their teaching—although I'm sure their presence still shapes more of my own teaching than I even realize—as it was in their shattering the boundaries that so often limit a young Christian's approach to the Bible. The unintended message in many discipleship programs is that the Bible is too complex to be read as a whole; and when it *is* read it needs to have the priest-like supervision of a study guide. I thank God that Art, Sam, and Jack had their own enormous appetites for the Word filled in a far more direct and robust format than that! It's with that contrast in mind that we move to the next chapter to meet John and Way.

4

Discovering the Bible
for Yourself

My experience of meeting God on the hillside at Clydehurst Christian Ranch in Montana was a prelude to watching God introduce himself to others. Some of these were friends who were already Christians, but who hadn't turned whatever corner there is in becoming deeply devoted to God. When the corner is turned, it's exciting to watch. I was able to "be there" on two occasions when God spoke through his Word as profoundly to others as he had to me. This assured me that anyone can draw closer to God by discovering the Bible—and God through it—just as I had. Johnny and Way are two of these men.

Johnny, the Other Christian

I met John the day I checked into Fort Myer, Virginia, as a recent draftee and now a newly minted military policeman. I had been posted to an elite MP company at the post that borders the Arlington Cemetery, next to the Pentagon. Twenty-seven generals lived on the small post, and our main job was to be sure they were properly

63

saluted as they came and went. But my biggest concern on arriving had little to do with measuring up to the demands of military pomp and circumstance. I needed to find some Christian fellowship as soon as possible.

The company clerk who checked me into the unit helped get me started with a brief comment.

"I see you graduated from Multnomah School of the Bible—are you a Christian?"

"You bet!" I responded, hopefully.

"Well, what the . . ." he swore in mild surprise. "You've been assigned to platoon six, with John, the other Christian in our company."

The other Christian? In a company of nearly 120 soldiers! It was a disappointing start, but I was happy to pursue the contact. I was knocking on Johnny's door within the hour.

"Hello, John, I'm new here. I was told that you're a Christian; is that right?"

He hesitated, looked around, and said, "Well, ah, yes I am."

"Great! So am I. I've been assigned to the platoon—my room is just up the hall."

After a brief exchange I asked, "Do you have a church yet?"

"Ah, no, not yet. I've only been here for a few weeks so I haven't had a chance to go looking yet—I hope to get to it pretty soon."

"How about this Sunday?"

When I knocked on his door that Sunday Johnny had forgotten church and had a tennis match already arranged with another MP, John Bulasko. That night, when I went to the evening service, he was playing Ping-Pong with another friend. Eventually we made connections and found a church that we both appreciated. We were also able to move off post and rent an apartment together. That was great for maintaining regular contact because I soon switched Army jobs—moving to a regular day shift—while Johnny continued as an MP on a rotating-shift schedule.

I soon realized that Johnny was struggling because of pressures from friends in the platoon. They were, in fact, glued together by their rotating shift. That scrambled any regular involvement for Johnny in Sunday worship, reducing his fellowship with other Christians. He also experienced a policeman's camaraderie that comes with the necessary reserve of police work; with it came a tendency to stay aloof from others when away from work. Thus the challenge for Johnny was to maintain his faith and to be accepted by his Army buddies at the same time—he was well-liked and wanted to keep it that way. The platoon's off-duty entertainments, though, tended towards creative unwholesomeness. Johnny refused to participate, but it didn't stop Bulasko and the others from badgering him to join them.

One morning at breakfast, after he had worked a swing shift the night before and I was getting ready for work, Johnny complained about the "persecution" he was experiencing. We had talked on a number of occasions about the pressures the men were putting on him but that didn't make much difference; he was becoming more and more of a martyr in his own eyes. He was also frustrated that I was showing less and less sympathy. I finally reacted.

"Johnny," I steamed, "it's because you don't stand for anything! You say you believe in God, but you never spend time with him." I asked him why he hardly ever read his Bible. In fact, I asked if he had ever read through the entire Bible. "If an infinite God gave us a book no bigger than this," I thumped my Bible down on the table, "it sure seems like it would be worthwhile reading! Your friends are just waiting for you to make up your mind about what you stand for...and so am I."

With that I left for work. My conscience, though, got to me right away—I'd been harsh and I was afraid I might have hurt our friendship. I came back to the apartment for lunch with an apology already formed, and hoped John would be home. He was. As I came in I started, "John, about this morning, I'm really sorr—"

He looked up and cut me off.

"Look Ron, don't apologize—I needed to hear it. And you know something, this is *good* stuff!" He was finishing Genesis after reading all morning. That evening he almost finished Exodus. It didn't end there. He read whenever he had time. He even started taking his Bible to work! As the radio dispatcher at the MP desk he had hours to spend reading magazines and novels, or talking with the other MPs as they came in and out.

Soon, in our apartment, he was telling me about the way the guys were responding to what he was reading to them from the Bible! I had a hard time picturing the scene, so one evening I showed up unannounced. As I arrived Johnny was reading a sharp warning from an Old Testament prophet to his friend and former problem, Bulasko.

"Man," Bulasko stammered, "I didn't know *that* was in there!"

"It sure is," John responded, "and you're in trouble, friend!" He had turned into a tiger.

Johnny not only gained new credibility with his MP friends (and ended the badgering), but also helped stimulate the young adult fellowship at our church. He completed his first read-through of the entire Bible in less than two months and, at the same time, began to have a remarkable impact on the lives of those close to him. This continued in the months that followed and was especially evident after he completed his military obligation. He wanted more time in the Bible, so he enrolled for a year of graduate studies at a Bible college—and a number of others from the group went with him! Just before he left I asked him about the impact the Bible was having on his life. "It made all the difference, Ron. Through the reading I fell in love with the Lord!"

Way, the Inquisitive Inquirer

Some years later Waymon, or Way as he preferred it, appeared at the singles ministry I was leading in a Boise church. He had also been in the Army so we had a couple of points in common, but his experience had been different from my own—namely alcohol, drugs, and a discharge. Before the Army he had lost his marriage to alcohol. Then he met Christ and started attending the church where I served as pastor of the singles group.

In our men's Bible study, Way soon caught my attention. He was usually very quiet, but at least once a meeting he would ask a question or two that the other men assumed were off limits: "Why doesn't God keep us from suffering if he loves us?" "If Jesus is God, why doesn't he know certain things?" and so on.

He had an honest appetite and an appetite for honesty! In time I decided to meet a requirement that each staff member have at least one person in a discipleship relationship by asking Way to team up with me. He accepted.

The main feature of our church discipleship program was a manual that borrowed the approach of multistep discipleship booklets used in various Christian organizations. What to do? Composing the manual had been the pet project of the pastoral staff, and the product promised certain benefits to anyone who used it. The problem was that I hadn't ever cared for discipleship manuals when I'd worked through them in other ministries. No matter how good they were, they lacked the power and attractiveness of the Bible itself. More than that, the student wasn't taught how to read the Bible in flow or to be self-fed from the Bible without an intermediary guide. That approach, I feared, might create a lasting impression that the Bible is largely inaccessible. Instead, I wanted Way to enjoy the discoveries of God's character as I had at Sechelt and Johnny had in Arlington.

The pastors agreed, hesitantly, to the proposal that Way and I would simply read through the Bible in a partnership—as long as we eventually got to the manual. We started and within a few weeks the same remarkable transition Johnny had evidenced began in Way's life. We met once a week for an hour or so, sharing, laughing, reading, and praying. This quiet, bruised man began to blossom out of the soil of his silence. On Sunday nights our 40 or so young adults met at a home for an open forum—a time when just one question would be entertained. For the rest of the evening we would work together to try to offer a useful Christian response. Issues could range from the nature of the hypostatic union to Christian values in dating.

It was on these evenings that Way's transformation was most obvious. The procedure for our discussions was to begin with personal responses and opinions and then to ask for any biblical content that related, shifting gears at about the halfway point of our seventy minutes. Hands were always flying up and voices loud during the "opinion" phase, but fewer knew where to go when we started to ask what God had to say on the subject. Way became the unassuming star of the second phase. "Well," he'd begin slowly, usually pulling at his wispy beard, "doesn't it say something about that in the book of

Numbers?" He'd then go on to make a point using a text about Moses or Aaron that very clearly applied to the issue at hand. The next week he'd mention content from places like Genesis, Leviticus, or Deuteronomy. Members of the group could be seen digging desperately through the unused pages of their Bibles or even looking to the index to find the books Way used—Amos, Hosea, Zechariah, Malachi, and so on. It wasn't a pompous parade of knowledge, either. Way was obviously excited about what he was sharing, and he gave illustrations from his own life about how a given scripture had touched him in recent days.

At first people were mystified about this young biblical guru in their midst—he hadn't had any formal Bible training, and was known to be a young Christian. I would smile as Way spoke, knowing that he was invariably sharing from a section of Scripture that we had gone over in our read-through partnership in recent days or weeks. Our exercise was soon common knowledge, though we hadn't promoted it. Even so, I was surprised when a pair of women approached me: "Just *what* is it that you two do when you meet? And how do you go about your reading? We'd like to do the same thing!" Soon we had about a dozen people meeting together in pairs to report to each other as part of their own Bible read-throughs.

It was about then that Nick arrived from California and joined our group. He was a recent high-school graduate and a new Christian. Like Way, Nick was full of questions. Most of all he wanted to know what he should do to grow in his newfound faith. I responded, "I suppose, as a starter, you can do what we're doing. Way and I are reading through the Bible in three months and we meet once a week to share some of what we've read."

"I'd love to do that too." Like me, Nick had come to faith by reading his Bible.

I approached Way, who was then nearing the New Testament in his own reading. "Would you be willing to meet a second time each week, Way, and take on Nick as another partner?" Way agreed, as long as he could just continue in the location of his own reading at that point and have Nick start with Genesis. That was fine, because the point of the reading wasn't to try to compare notes on the same content. The real goal was to make sure he would be well nourished by the Word. Indeed, within a few weeks Nick almost matched his mentor's enthusiasm in offering Bible content at our Forum sessions.

All that took place in 1976. Since then Way has worked on a ranch, ministered in rural churches, and continues to read through his Bible, still taking people with him. Nick is now a missionary and wrote to me not long ago, "Well, Ron, I just finished another round!"

5

Bible Discipleship—Reading, Sharing, Growing

Leszek, my translator, startled me. I was in the middle of telling the Army story—of the time Johnny told me that he had come to love God through reading the Bible. I was used to the rhythm of speaking with a translator; I would offer a sentence or two and he would match me with his sentence or two in Polish, pause, and look at me, which was his cue for me to continue. But now Leszek was off and running with his own message!

We were at a seminary on the outskirts of Warsaw, speaking to the youth leaders from three evangelical denominations in Poland. These were the cream of the emerging evangelical church in Poland—a youthful cadre of dedicated believers who were learning to lead others in their walk with Christ. The 35 individuals had come from throughout the country. No matter their small number, they were a strategic group. The process of multiplication had taken a group of 12 men under Christ (adding Matthias in place of Judas Iscariot) to turn the Mediterranean world upside down within a few decades of Christ's ascension. Similarly, Paul began with 12 poorly taught men in

Ephesus and worked with them for three years. Paul offered them "the whole purpose of God" (Acts 20:27)—the truths of the Christian gospel—in a multiplying ministry that impacted all of West Asia, so much so that it led to a riot! In the city of Ephesus, the commerce centered on the worship of Diana had collapsed after just three years of ministry by Paul. Thus, with 35 dedicated Polish Christians, we were well on our way.

Leszek finally paused and explained to me what he was saying. "Ron, I was just telling them how important it is that they read their Bibles—we will never fall in love with God if we don't get to know him. I told them that I was committing myself to begin reading through the Bible this very day and was challenging them to do the same!"

The next morning, one of the members of the Josiah Venture team—the missionaries who sponsored the conference—shared with me that well after midnight he had dropped in on one of the rooms to see what the four Poles were doing up that late at night. They were reading their Bibles! Partnerships had been formed and a number of the conferees had committed to reading through the whole Bible in the next few months, with Leszek leading the way.

An article I wrote for *Moody Monthly* magazine years earlier had been translated into Polish by some of the missionaries, and the basic steps suggested in the article were being used to guide these budding read-through partnerships. In this chapter, we're going to look at these steps in detail.

The Elements of a Read-through Partnership

Bible discipleship is a partnership that features a life-to-life sharing of truths drawn from each person's weekly Bible reading. A partnership needs at least two people, and usually no more than three. The central task is simple:

the partners agree to read through the Bible, on their own, at a fast pace. As they read, they underline verses that stand out to them (for any reason). Then, during a weekly meeting, they select some of those underlined verses to read to their partner, with each person given just ten minutes to read as many verses as the time allows. This isn't a time for explanations or questions—*just reading!* The block of time given to the mutual readings should, however, be couched in some natural sharing and prayer so that the meeting involves other elements of fellowship. But it pivots on the readings, which must *always* be honored—the shared verses represent God's voice within the fellowship.

As simple as the Bible read-through partnership may be, it will still be useful to walk through each element, step by step.

1. The Invitation

No one comes to a party unless they're invited! A reading partnership needs someone to take the initiative. Don't wait for someone else to step forward—pray for a candidate, and then start looking for the answer.

Who might you start with? One possibility is your spouse. A partnership in the Word is a good way to open your souls to each other, sharing what God has underlined in your lives during the week. You may want this to be part of a weekly "date." It's good to consider other options as well—this isn't an either/or dilemma, since the same reading can be reviewed twice. In my tracking of read-throughs the greatest returns usually come in same-gender teams. The exercise can quickly become a soul-to-soul experience even if personality profiles might not match in other ways. In fact, there are really just three crucial elements to good partnerships: a shared *appetite* to grow spiritually; a shared *commitment* to meet; and a *completion date* that both partners affirm as challenging but realistic.

Sean, a graduate student at our seminary, is my current reading partner. At our recent end-of-the-year student retreat I spoke, sharing with the students how significant Bible-reading partnerships have been for me. A few days later Sean approached me and asked whether I'd be open to doing a Bible read-through with him. I was surprised and pleased by his appetite to be involved in a Bible-centered activity, something not all seminary students are ready for after a year of hard academic work!

I knew Sean better than most of my students because he had been in some of my classes and had served as a leader in the Masters' Cabinet, a student leadership group I worked with. How soon did he want to begin? He answered, "Right away!" The adventure had begun. I asked him what pace he wanted to pursue. He hesitated. Maybe two months, or three, he suggested. I asked whether he'd be ready to invest a lot of his discretionary time to the reading. He said yes. So a two-month pace *was* possible. But I wasn't able to match that pace; I was also committed to my writing, to professional reading, to preparation of a new course for the fall, and to summer committee work that goes with my job. I suggested we aim at a completion date at the end of the summer. He agreed.

Since our first agreement we've had two meetings, each taking between 40 minutes and an hour. His mornings are free as mine are, so we agreed to meet each Friday at 9:00 A.M. in my office. Each meeting began with a time of sharing what was happening in our lives. This past week, for instance, I talked about my deep concern for a member of our church who had lost the fingers on one of his hands in a work accident. I felt inadequate in responding to the crisis but had learned from others in my trying to help. Sean then shared about his struggle with a post-school-year letdown that undermined his motivation to do a number of things he wants to accomplish. The sharing took about 20 minutes; then we read our underlined scriptures to each other. It was his turn to go first, for eight to ten minutes. Then I followed with my own verses for the same length of time. We closed with prayers about what we had just read and prayers for the things we had shared earlier. It was a *very* encouraging time, and this was just our second meeting.

As you approach a candidate, make sure you've assessed his or her appetite for God's Word, the availability of a practical time and place for meeting, and a pace that both of you can maintain. Because you are the one reading this book, most likely you will be the one who initiates the partnership. Raise the prospect of a reading partnership as a possibility, without saying anything that might make the other person feel guilty if he or she isn't interested, able, or ready. My best experiences have come from a partner who asks hard but genuine questions and who appreciates whatever learning opportunities the church might provide. Often I find that those who desire an active role in ministry or who can be trusted with a ministry are the type who would want to do a read-through of the Bible. As Jesus said recalling John 8:31,47, a "true disciple" will have a desire for the Word that isn't ever satiated, whether young or old in his or her faith. That's not to say that every devoted Christian will leap at a read-through opportunity when it's offered, but they do make the best candidates.

I'll plant seeds—"broadcasting"—either by sharing with a group of Christians, or with individuals, about my experience with Bible-reading partnerships. Sean is a good example of how broadcasting works, even to the point that he was the initiator in our current read-through commitment. Sharing about read-throughs is just the first stage of a process. If a man I respect seems like a candidate I'll find a time to tell him my story, including some specifics about the way the partnership works and the benefits it offers. The first contact can be a breakfast, or part of an ongoing contact at church. All that's needed is enough time to explain the approach.

Offering this book to browse for a week or two would be a good starter. Then plant a specific seed: "So, Steve, I'm thinking about starting a read-through in a couple of weeks—I'd love to team up with you if you're interested. Check out your calendar and I'll touch base with you next week." Whether Steve is hesitant or ready to jump at it, I'll wait a week or so before asking for a response or commitment. People need time to think about a challenge, especially if it's demanding. It also gives the Spirit time to stir their priorities.

Don't be pessimistic! I've discovered that lots of folks—even those who seem terribly busy—are looking for a challenge they count worthwhile. As we've seen already, busyness is really a matter of priorities: We always find a way to do what we think is important! Indeed, some of my most avid partners have been men with lives already full to overflowing—from successful businessmen in Chicago and Portland, to fellow students in the midst of very demanding academic programs in Portland, Chicago, and London.

Don't be surprised at how ready a person might be to make a commitment; especially when you're a person he appreciates. You're telling him that you're willing to invest your own time in working *with* him. The world doesn't offer many opportunities for weekly meetings that have the depth and benefit this can offer. Even if he can't or won't make a commitment now, you've given him a challenge to think about and a compliment—namely, that you were ready to team up in a high-commitment exercise because he commanded *your* respect.

2. The Contract

When someone agrees in principle to begin a read-through, you need to make sure you both agree on the format, the time and place of meeting, and the completion date. The format, of course, is generally understood already, based on the seed-planting and recruitment presentations. But it still helps to actually do a brief practice exercise in which you show exactly what is expected. For instance, with Sean I demonstrated what my part of the Scripture sharing time would be like in the following week by selecting underlined verses from my current reading. I simply read four or five verses verbatim and said, "That's it—nothing more to it! We each get about ten minutes to cover as many verses as we can." This reassures the partner that there isn't some hidden agenda—some expectation that the passages need to be explained or a justification made for the selections. It's the "keep it simple" method applied with a passion.

I've found that if I don't illustrate the "reading-and-nothing-more" approach, the new partner will usually come with an expectation that it can't be *this* simple and still be useful. He will often assume, instead, that some kind of deeper dialogue is necessary. It's true, of course, that when the verse-sharing is completed, some in-depth discussions about life issues are likely to arise. The point to remember is that any subsequent conversation is stimulated and enriched in important ways by the Bible-reading, and the conversation must not displace reading the text itself.

On occasions when someone tells me they've tried a read-through with a partner but it failed, I'll ask whether they were careful to observe the time for mutual verse sharing. That usually proves to be the problem—they may read their Bibles during the week and meet to share summarized insights and personal experiences of the week, but fail to guard time for reviewing their underlined verses. The meetings go forward for a few weeks but the sense of benefit begins to dry up rather than increase—the insights just aren't as crisp or productive as those in the text itself, and the sharing may descend into ordinary chatting that's hard to justify in a busy world. God's Word offers a transcendent element and his voice makes all the difference in any conversation!

Agreement on time and place would seem to be simple enough, but there can be pitfalls if we don't make sure the meeting circumstances are secure and stable. With my schedule I discovered, for instance, that meetings on Fridays or weekends aren't particularly wise because of the number of times I am out of town for weekend speaking engagements or other travel obligations. If you find that a time isn't working out, rescheduling can be a solution. Whatever the case, you both need to affirm the meetings are a high priority.

To illustrate the problem of priorities, I recall a dear friend, Larry, who felt our meeting times could serve double-duty as a chance to do laundry, using the inexpensive machines at my dormitory, while we met! That seemed fine in principle, but in practice Larry was usually distracted by the need to switch his clothes from the washer to the dryer midway through our time together. He knew that the machines were in constant use, and if he didn't switch his clothes, someone else would dump them who knows where, or would get one of the better dryers Larry needed in order to have the laundry all done by the time we finished. This arrangement just didn't work. In exasperation, I stopped dropping mild hints and got right to the point: "Look Larry, I'm happy to meet with you at midnight, at five in the morning, or any other time we can carve out...but *please*, let's make sure we have quality time for this—it's silly for us to play second fiddle to your laundry!" He graciously agreed to new laundry arrangements, and we carried on in fine fashion.

Midweek breakfasts may be the most practical choice for a sharing time. The advantages are obvious. It doesn't take away from family times, and it allows for a weekly rhythm, usually without as many competing events as other times of a day. Lunch hour can also serve well for partners who are in the same part of town, or in a shared business or school environment. There are drawbacks, though, for meeting times that involve meals. It can be a bit clumsy to share your heart with someone while they peel an egg or unpack a cup of yogurt. And if you meet in a restaurant, you may find it awkward when you're sharing something very personal, only to notice that the people in the next booth have stopped talking because they're listening in on your conversation! Then there are the interruptions that might come from the waiter. When it comes to meeting together, private and quiet works best.

Sometimes partners will find it necessary to be somewhat flexible about the meeting time. For example, mothers with preschool children have time challenges that make it difficult to find *any* time that is certain to be stable—unless someone else helps out or reasonable child care is available.

All this to say that the time and place of meeting calls for some foresight and a commitment to finding an environment that works as well as possible for uninterrupted sharing. Some creative thinking may be needed, but the rewards will be worth the investment!

3. The Pace

The commitment to a completion date will dictate the reading pace. If, for instance, a reading partnership aims to complete a read-through in a year, the partners need to average a bit more than three chapters a day. Two cycles can be completed in a year by reading a bit under seven chapters a day. A faster pace is certainly possible; Christian writer Philip Yancey, for instance, once read through the entire Bible in one week while hiding away in a Colorado mountain cabin. My fastest tour of the Bible, which took about six weeks, was laggardly by comparison.

Yancey's pace is, of course, the road less traveled. Why? Is it unusually difficult to read at that pace? Perhaps for some, but there are many who enjoy reading who will devour novels the size of the Bible in two or three weeks without giving it a thought. The issue, once again, is really one of priorities. Most of us just aren't ready to use that much of our discretionary time on Bible reading.

Another reason for a slower tempo in Bible reading—among those who make daily Bible reading a habit—is, no doubt, the strength of the tradition of meditative Bible reading. Those from the meditative tradition savor books and passages in the Bible as treasures and are willing to reflect carefully about possible meanings and applications. Why, then, read at a pace that overwhelms such benefits? Isn't the fast-paced Bible reader a bit like a man trying to drink the spray from a hose while ignoring a nearby glass of iced tea?

Not really. The two approaches are *not* in competition as "either-or" options, but are mutually supportive. One is like a month-long drive across the United States, stopping to enjoy many scenic outlooks and wonderful parks along the way. The other is like taking a jet that leaves Seattle in the morning, flies at 33,000 feet, and arrives in Miami about four hours later. Both approaches have their benefits!

The assumptions that support the Bible read-through are affirmed by Jesus in his dialogue with a certain Cleopas and his friend on the road to Emmaus. This was just after the resurrection. The two men, presumably adequate in their knowledge of the Hebrew Scriptures as were the other disciples, were scolded by Christ for not having an accurate synthetic overview of the Bible: "O foolish men and slow of heart to believe in all that the prophets have spoken!" Jesus went on and, "beginning with Moses and with all the prophets, He explained to them the things concerning Himself in all the Scriptures" (Luke 24:25,27). Here Jesus assumes that crucial issues such as a biblical Christology were not an option for disciples but an expectation. He expected them to have an astute understanding of how the Bible fits together, and about the substance of all the elements, including the first five books of the Bible, which Moses wrote, and "the prophets" which we assume was his inclusive category for the balance of the Hebrew Scriptures. Such knowledge cannot be won with a single pass through the Bible!

The read-through pace also offers the reader a chance to see the message of the Bible in overview, thus offering a context for many immediate issues. For instance, the reader of the New Testament book of Hebrews will have a much more effective grasp of the writer's arguments if he has just read the priestly instructions of the Old Testament a few days or even a couple of months earlier. In fact, the faster the Bible is read, the more impact the New Testament's use of the Old Testament will have for the reader. The reason that Paul or James quoted the Old Testament was to create an impact that an informed reader would find compelling. The biblical Christian, as he or she matures, must rise to that expectation in the text, or else run the risk of isolating specific New Testament texts from their important theological antecedents.

More important, however, is the benefit that comes to a reader in discovering the "personality" of God that begins to emerge in a fast-paced reading. God's inspiration of the various Bible authors—the *sensus plenior,* or "full sense" of the Word—tends to remain a technical theological point until a reader begins to be captured by the emerging character of the Person who moves throughout the text. God's compassion and lovingkindness become living qualities, not just concepts. He begins to capture and refresh the believer in ways that can't be adequately described.

4. Marking the Text

The genius of the read-through approach is its simplicity as we embrace our relationship with God through it. In the Bible God offers his own words in the most direct, distinct, and reliable manner possible, short of Christ's return. The Bible *is* his Word—the collected treasure of the very words he moved the biblical authors to write, words sent to disclose his ways and accomplish his remarkable purposes among us.

The task of the read-through participant is simply to underline verses that stand out to him as he reads. No agenda is needed other than the agenda the Spirit might have as he underlines verses in the heart of the receptive reader. The goal is to respond to the Scripture as a true listener, and not so much as an analyst. By receiving permission to underline whatever catches their attention, for whatever reasons, readers are able to follow the contours of the text more freely than if their goal is to mine it for certain truths or lessons. There's a time and place, of course, for guided research, but it isn't a goal of read-through discipleship.

Think of the read-through exercise as sitting before God, just listening, like the throngs who listened to Jesus on the Galilean hillsides. On those occasions it was God's agenda that defined what the people heard. On other occasions, such as the times when Jesus was alone with his disciples, he invited them to ask their questions—to "study" topics they were interested in learning about. So both approaches have their place; but the read-through is meant to offer us a chance to sit, listen, and respond in the simplest manner possible. That's what makes it work so well—the pressures of analysis, synthesis, and making judgments are left in the background. The exercise of marking the Bible is the basic work of gaining knowledge and understanding, while growing in areas that call for application.

Some readers might be more involved than others in their verse-underlining. Should dozens of verses in a given chapter be underlined? There aren't any rules here. After all, it's a personal exercise of choosing. But there will only be ten or so minutes to report a week's worth of underlining to the other person, so some restraint in the text-marking will help make some things stand out more clearly when that time comes. For instance, I average just one or two verses (or clusters of related verses) a chapter during my read-throughs.

A pair of brief digressions are in order here. First, the issue of marking Bibles. Some readers may be hesitant to underline verses in their Bibles, respecting the fact that it's the Word of God. I believe that's a mistaken application of honor. God's purpose in offering us his Word is to build a relationship with him. Marking the Bible is an expression of pursuing God—seeking to know him better. In time, the printed pages of our personal Bibles will yellow and turn brittle with age. It's better that we wear them out by vigorous use, isn't it?

Then there's the problem of doing a second or third read-through in the same Bible. Certain passages will catch the reader's attention just as much the second and third time through as they did the first time. These will have to be marked a different way if they've already been marked once, such as by using brackets around a verse, or placing a check mark next to the text. Sometimes I'll use a particular color of ink for a given read-through. Whatever the case, the matter of repetition is not a problem because it's encouraging to rediscover verses to the point that they become easy to paraphrase or summarize, and even to memorize. So, let the pen or pencil help you focus—mark, mark, and mark again.

5. The Weekly Meeting

The weekly meeting offers a chance to join others in listening to God speak. It's the relational payoff for reading during the week. Each participant has the opportunity to hear what was underlined in the text and heart of the other member. But more than that, it gives God, the ultimate author of the Bible, a voice in the meeting. It's amazing how frequently Bible verses can stir the soul, reminding the readers of God's grace or greatness. The Scriptures have even more power when they are read and understood within their original context.

C. S. Lewis captured the genius of the weekly meeting in his discussion of friendships in *The Four Loves*. There, Lewis suggests that the richness of ordinary friendship is in its camaraderie around a shared pleasure. Whereas romantic love is characterized by the face-to-face encounter, the joy of friendships is found in being shoulder-to-shoulder, gazing together at a common delight. For the believer who is already captured by God's greatness, or is growing to enjoy the truths about God in the Bible, there is more pleasure to be found in the partnership of looking to God than one might imagine. This delight is never selfish or exclusive. Instead, there is a deep enjoyment in inviting others to participate. In friendships, the greater the significance of a shared pleasure, the richer the fellowship. If a team of hikers, for instance, conquer a daunting mountain, the bonding of their shared challenge and fascination will be sustained for years to come. How much more the bond of sitting together at the feet of the God of all glory!

The weekly meeting should begin with the normal exchanges of a friendship. Life brings a set of challenges and opportunities every day; in a week there's a lot to sort through. The chance to take some time to report what is happening in our lives is crucial to the fabric of relationships. The man or woman who remembers a sensitive sidebar of the last time together, and asks about it, is giving worth to the one who is asked. We trust others when we know they care for us and remember the small as well as the larger matters of life. Also, a number of the things shared during the first 15 or 20 minutes together will become the content of the partners' prayers after the Bible verses are reported.

Depending on what's agreed upon, the exchange of weekly verses needs to begin with enough time to avoid feeling rushed, and with enough time left for praying together—which is the natural response to the exchange of life-news and the sharing of verses. The verse exchange can be handled any way the participants desire, but the simplest approach usually works best in such things. In my experience, the ideal is to allow each participant a limited amount of time to share as many verses as possible in the time allotted. I will start sharing my verses, for instance, and continue until I reach the ten-minute mark, when my time is up. The next person then shares for ten minutes, and so on if there are more than two in the group. The length of time devoted to the verse exchange is arbitrary, of course, but ten minutes feels about right. It allows quite a few verses to be shared but feels rushed enough to limit the casual chatter and theological digressions that easily slip in.

The call to guard the verse-sharing time from other kinds of discussion is very important, as we've noted before. Again, the most common reason some Bible-reading partnerships fail is because the participants are not disciplined about how they use their time. Many of us have a tendency to talk about things that seem terribly important at the moment, but if measured by memory a week later, turn out to be much less scintillating. If, for instance, my calendar is as crowded as ever when the day comes to have the second or third meeting of my read-through partnership, I'll probably ask whether the weekly meeting is *really* worthwhile. If I look back to the prior meeting and only remember my partner trying to explain to me his latest insight into predestination and the sovereignty of God, I might decide I have something better to do. Or, again, if the entire time was spent talking about a failed dating relationship, my priorities might not support continuing. By contrast, God's Word has remarkable staying power. If both readers are at all hungry to grow spiritually, then the commitment to exchange verses for 20 minutes during the middle of the meeting time will be the magnet drawing both members together, while keeping the meeting time focused.

The Fruit of read-through Partnerships

Recently I met with Dave, who is from a large Portland-area church. We were working out some specific arrangements for a weeknight class I will be teaching in the fall. As we wrapped up our discussion he offered me a special encouragement.

"Did you hear," he asked, "about the impact your Bible-reading article had in our church?"

"No," I responded, "but I knew it had been included as a bulletin insert a few months ago." Alan, one of the pastors, had asked me for permission to use the article, and I was delighted to agree to it. The church offers six separate services each weekend, so this meant a good number of people would be introduced to the concept of Bible discipleship. Afterwards, though, I didn't hear anything more about it.

"It seems that a number of people decided to team up and read through the Bible after that sermon—lots of folks just did it on their own initiative. I decided to ask if any of the men in my fellowship group wanted to team up with me this summer, and I got a volunteer. The man who agreed to team up with me had been growing spiritually—asking lots of good questions in the group. Anyway, he was a great candidate for it. He put his heart into it and charged ahead, even when I lagged behind. He finished in just 90 days!"

After that, Dave shared, the man started up yet another Bible read-through, this time on his own. Dave reiterated how much the man was growing, even though the man himself wasn't particularly aware of the changes taking place in his life. In fact, the man was able, offhand, to summarize the landscape of the entire Bible, but didn't think much about it.

Dave asked him, "Would you have been able to do that a year ago?" Only then did it dawn on the man that the Bible was now much more alive to him—a part of his life in a way it had never been before. He had grown and changed, but it wasn't something he noticed as it happened. But from what Dave shared, it was pretty obvious to others.

That's the way Bible reading works; it feeds our souls, drawing the "eyes of our hearts" upward as we open ourselves to the mind of Christ in a bolder way than ever before. We begin to grow in the process, and others see it even if we don't see it ourselves. That's the way real growth works, isn't it?

6

The Landscape of the Bible

On my first full day in Israel I left Tel Aviv for Galilee. Until then, Galilee was just a name from childhood Bible stories. This trip changed all that. After traveling along the coastal plain north of Tel Aviv for an hour, the bus turned in a more eastward direction and began to climb a moderate grade, twisting through the surrounding hills. After a few miles we began our descent, still turning through the hilly terrain until we came to a major intersection. Before us was a broad valley. To our right was a military camp stirring with Israeli soldiers, and next to it a prison for captured Syrian soldiers. On our left was a large, scarred mound, almost a quarter-mile long, carved at many points by decades of archaeological digs.

This hill, I realized, had to be the ancient city of Megiddo, a strategic site throughout history. The main highway of the fertile crescent—that vast watered region which cradled early civilization, stretching from Egypt northward to Iraq—was forced through this narrow pass. The valley that spread out before us was linked to Megiddo in the Bible as the site of the promised battle of Armageddon (from a Semitic phrase meaning "Mount Megiddo"). King Solomon made Megiddo one of his main fortified cities in biblical times. The Bible also reports that King Josiah died here trying to block an Egyptian army, led by Pharaoh Neco, from traveling through the pass. More recently, during World War I, General Allenby of Great Britain captured the pass in a move that displaced Ottoman rule in the region. As our bus paused at the intersection, a squat, Russian-made tank from Syria crossed in front of us on a low-slung transporter. It must have been captured on the Golan battlefields just a few dozen miles away. The crossing road was the major east-west route connecting the Jordan Valley with Haifa on the Mediterranean coast.

That intersection made the Bible come alive for me in a startling new way. The kibbutz I would join lay on the north-central edge of this broad valley—the Jezreel Valley—almost at the base of Mount Tabor. It was from Tabor that some of the tribes of Israel, under the leadership of Deborah and Barak, battled the Canaanites under Sisera. As the Bible story unfolds in Judges 4–5, it mentions the "ancient torrent, the torrent of the Kishon." We passed over the Kishon soon after leaving the Megiddo intersection. It was a mild stream; but my mind's eye could envision a day long ago when thundering clouds had unleashed massive rains which quickly filled the river basin and overflowed into the valley. This wild Kishon limited the ability of the Canaanite chariots—the tanks of Deborah's day—to concentrate their forces. Even the individual chariots quickly bogged down in muddy fields. The Israelites, without chariots of their own, saw their providential opportunity. With a signal from Barak, the Israelite soldiers began to descend from the steep slopes of Tabor, where they had camped beyond the range of the chariots. Now they were able to slog through the fields on equal terms with their dismounted enemies, and they soon succeeded in routing the Canaanites.

The bus dropped me off at Dovrat, near the base of Mount Tabor, at the north end of the ancient battlefield. This was to be my new home for the months to come. During my early days at Dovrat, another war raged. For a time the cease-fire of the October 1973 war failed to stop the shelling by Syrians and Israelis on the Golan Heights. From my kibbutz I could hear the distant "thumps" of shells exploding. Israel, I realized, was a very small, dramatic, and volatile place!

The landscape of the Bible had first been portrayed to me by Art, my youth pastor in Spokane. It's not that Art had ever been to Israel, but he did have a clear view of the internal landscape—not only the physical geography, but the geography of ideas and events in biblical history. In our weekly Bible study that met in Sonny's house on Ash Street, Art explained to us that the Bible is bound together by a set of themes. The varied books, letters, and poems recorded or reflected events guided by God. The Bible writers were superintended by God to explain his purposes and values in directing those events. Art coached us in every type of landscape as we traced the themes of sin and grace, fall and redemption, while we occasionally looked at Bible maps to see where the events we were reading about had taken place. Since then I've continued to develop a more vivid picture of God's working in history—through studies, travels, and my Bible reading. This chapter offers an overview of what to expect.

Major Bible Themes

The Bible is especially jolting to unwary readers who are used to the flow and effective transitions of well-crafted, modern-day books. Even to a reader who knows what to expect, the Bible is disjointed at many points. Unless the main themes and structure are known, a reader may be tempted to avoid certain sections, especially in the Old Testament. A tendency among Christians is to read a few "favorite" sections and ignore the rich benefits to be found in the less reader-friendly parts of Scripture. Some help is offered by Bible publishers who add introductory comments, books, interpretive headings, and sidebar commentaries. But a more fundamental orientation is needed in order to begin a productive read-through of the whole Bible. Knowing the central themes is most important for appreciating the overall content, and knowing the historical and literary structures is most useful in helping to see how any part fits into the whole.

Art, my high-school youth pastor, and Sam, the retired Canadian missionary, and Jack, who founded Multnomah Bible College, all had a crucial part in helping me to see the continuity of the Bible. Art pointed to the "red ribbon" of God's plan to resolve sin. The theme of salvation is central to Christ's life. But salvation is always linked to sin—always in a disease-and-cure symmetry. Sam helped me see the role of trees in raising and solving the problem of sin. Another theme is one of warning, punishment, and restoration—the exile theme. Our survey of key biblical themes, then, will feature the red ribbon, the exile and return, and the biblical trees.

1. The Red Ribbon

Genesis is the first book of the Bible. Of its 50 chapters, only the first two portray a world without sin. From chapter three until near the end of the final book in the New Testament, Revelation, we're faced with a world enslaved to the curse of sin and death. The very brief window we have of a sinless world is fascinating and promising. The creation was evaluated by God and declared in each part to be "good" and the whole was "very good." This goodness implied warm companionship between God and creation. Work, portrayed as man's dominion over "every living thing that moves on the earth," was accomplished from the headquarters of a beautiful and fruitful garden (see Genesis 1:28-30). It was an idyllic setting until sin appeared. The serpent who introduced sin by tempting Adam and Eve to eat fruit from the tree of the knowledge of good and evil, despite God's prohibition, is ultimately responsible for the fall. It is the serpent's fate—his eventual death—that introduces the red ribbon.

A ribbon isn't actually suggested in the Bible, of course, but the imagery is very effective in capturing God's progressive solution to sin—a solution woven through biblical history. The ribbon has a distinct beginning and end. Thus, the Bible makes it clear that the problem of evil is transitional, a problem God addresses before believers enter into eternal life with Christ.

I was introduced to this imagery in a wide-page "Panorama" Bible-study course that Art sometimes brought to our high-school study.[1] The illustrations in the book were all black and white, with gray shading. That made its chief feature stand out—a large, bright red ribbon-like line that extended through each page. This red ribbon connected people, places, and events to show the progression of God's promise throughout history.

The first circle was "The Promise" of Genesis 3:15, and the final circle led to the events of the final judgment at the end of the present historical era. In between were figures such as Seth, Noah, Shem, Abram, Isaac, Jacob (or Israel, as he was renamed), Moses, David, and so on. The chief figure was Jesus, pictured on the cross as the penultimate figure on the ribbon.

---

1. Alfred T. Eade, *The "Panorama" Bible Study Course: Plan of the Ages* (Old Tappan, NJ: Revell, 1947).

This floppy-paged book helped me see how all the particulars of the Bible are ultimately bound together by a theme: God addressed the problem of sin by sending his Son, thus fulfilling his promise to Adam and his related promise of blessing to Abraham. This theme is present in various forms or stages in most parts of the Bible and ties them together. Its portrayal of Jesus Christ makes him the pivotal figure of history and reminds us of Paul's teaching in Ephesians 1, where the apostle explains that it was God's "kind intention" (Ephesians 1:5), planned long ago by God, to orchestrate all the dimensions of time and space so that all things are summed up in Christ. Thus, our response to the biblical teachings about Christ are the central concern of life.

Here are the locations where God's promise, finally fulfilled in Jesus, are found.[2]

Figure 1: **The Promise Theme**

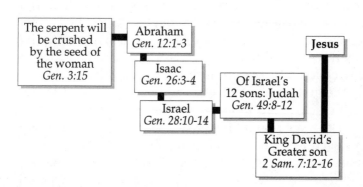

---

2. See Walter C. Kaiser's development of this theme in *Toward a Biblical Theology* (Grand Rapids: Zondervan, 1978).

The crushed serpent. The serpent appears in Genesis chapter 3 without much explanation. The serpent is described as "crafty," and its willingness to challenge God's character and word makes it clear that the serpent has already embraced evil and become its guiding advocate. In Revelation 20:2 the serpent is identified as "the devil and Satan," so the titles are interchangeable. According to Ezekiel, Satan originally was a beautiful cherub, created as a bejeweled honor guard in God's heavenly throneroom (28:11-14). Evil began with Satan's decision to look away from God to gaze at his own beauty. This narcissistic fascination with self burst into a malignant self-love and a declaration of independence from God, which led to Satan's downfall (Ezekiel 28:15-19). The title *Satan* is actually a description, meaning "adversary"—one who continually finds fault with God and man.

As God entered the garden in the Genesis 3 narrative he immediately addressed the problem of sin with a series of questions and judgments. When God questioned Adam about his sin, man pointed to Eve as the source of his problem. Eve, in turn, blamed the serpent for deceiving her. God accepted her charge as legitimate and responded by grace in a symmetrical solution to their sin: If the deceived woman, Eve, was an unwitting agent through which the serpent worked, so also a woman would be the agent through whom God would work to defeat the serpent's scheme.

God projected two future progenies who will emerge throughout history—namely, the seed of the serpent and the seed of the woman. The two will be in perpetual opposition until the serpent is defeated. The "seed" of the woman is a curious expression, if the biological realities (understood then as now) are considered, and seems to anticipate the uniqueness of Christ's virgin birth. God promised that "he"—portraying the woman's seed as a single individual—will eventually crush the serpent's head. That edict makes the point that the seed of the serpent will not be distinguished from the serpent himself when the future judgment comes: It is the serpent himself whose head will be crushed and, implicitly, so will his progeny.

This "battle of the seeds" is the context for the rest of the Bible; it sets up a perpetual polarity of Satan's rebellion and God's solution. It is here that the "promise" of God's solution begins. It will be an expensive solution, leaving the woman's singular seed with a crushed heel—which will be fulfilled, as we discover at the end of the ribbon, by the death of Jesus Christ through the machinations of the serpent. The blood of Christ colors the ribbon red.

As I said earlier, the "Panorama" study that Art shared in our high-school Bible study contained many more names than the brief set offered in Figure 1. The reason for the very short list I've given is that it accentuates the theme by pointing to the most conspicuous figures and notices their more explicit exposures to God's restated promise. The Old Testament, however, is actually very careful to keep track of the many additional figures through whom the promise travels through history. This is part of the importance of genealogies.

Adam and Eve, for instance, have three sons who receive special attention. More than three children were born to them, of course, but these three are crucial because of their role in portraying the progress of the promise. Cain is the firstborn and, in Genesis 4:1, it appears that Eve thinks he is the promised solution. By translating the Hebrew text very literally, we can understand Eve to be saying, "Look, I've birthed a man, *namely* Yahweh!" Cain, however, proved to be a murderer. He killed Abel, his younger and more faithful brother.

The promise-carrier, then, had to be someone else. That proves to be Seth, who is the "likeness" and "image" of his father Adam. The Bible reader will find it illuminating to trace this theme as it carries forward. Noah, for instance, became the sole keeper of the promise when God sent the flood to destroy the rest of humanity. Of his sons, Shem (the father of the eventual Semites) is selected over Ham and Japheth.

Abraham and his offspring. That takes us to Abram for a major shift in the development of the "promise" theme. To Abram God spoke of the promise as a "blessing" that God would offer to all of humanity through Abram's progeny, the future nation of Israel. "Promise" and "blessing" must be taken to be the same thing—namely, the solution to the problem of evil that the serpent, and his follower Adam, unleashed on the world.

The blessing offered to Abram was multifaceted, including God's promise that he would eventually become the father of a great nation and that he would gain a tremendous reputation. The part of the promise that pertains to us, though, is that Abram would become a blessing to others: "in you all the families of the earth shall be blessed" (Genesis 12:3).

This promise might seem a bit cryptic, leading a critic to ask, "Just how does this vague statement of blessing relate to the earlier promise that the head of the serpent would be crushed, or to an anticipation of Jesus, as your chart suggests?" That's a fair question. The answer is indirect: First, the pace and purpose of Genesis shifts very clearly with the appearance of Abram at the end of chapter 11. From that point onward the focus of the Bible is on Abram's clan. Before he appeared, the narrative raced forward with hundreds of years taken in quick leaps; suddenly in Genesis 12 the pace shifts so that

Abram's life and the next three generations of his family consume the remaining 38 chapters of the book.

Moses' reason for tracing Abram and his family at such length emerges through the selection of content. (Moses was the writer of the first five books of the Bible, otherwise known as the Pentateuch.) Moses clearly doesn't intend to offer a family biography—the content covered is far too sketchy for that. Instead, he explains how the blessing is passed along and how the problem of sin, and God's initiatives in dealing with sin, are at work in each generation. For instance, two stories of Abraham's (unsuccessful) willingness to share his wife with other men make it clear that he's not portrayed as a flawless hero. Instead, we discover that God patiently and persistently carries Abraham from a flawed faith to an exemplary faith—a faith that eventually is able to give his beloved son, Isaac, back to God in chapter 22. The theme of growing in faith is a constant throughout the Bible.

Similarly we find that Abraham's grandson, Jacob—later renamed Israel—is a man whose chief concern in life is self-advancement. By the time God is finished with him, we find a selfless man whose faith in God is exemplary. Then in the next generation we find another case of gross evil when Joseph, who first appears as Jacob's spoiled son, is treacherously sold by his brothers to be a slave in Egypt. Yet by the end of the story Joseph, blessed by God, has become the prime minister of Egypt and his brothers are under *his* rule! In Genesis 50:20 Joseph offers his brothers a reassurance that can also serve as a thematic summary of the entire book: "You meant evil against me, but God meant it for good in order to bring about this present result, to preserve many people [including our family] alive." That is, throughout Genesis the dark soil of human sin always served to bear flowers of faith and blessing under the supernatural care of God.

A second reason for seeing the promise of blessing in Genesis 12:1-3 to be pivotal to the entire message of the Bible is that it continues to be developed. As Figure 1 shows, the promise is restated to both Isaac and Israel. In Genesis 26:4 Isaac was told by God that "by your descendants all the nations of the earth shall be blessed." In Genesis 28:14 Isaac's son, Jacob, is told by God, "In you and in your descendants shall all the families of the earth be blessed." This promise, then, was hardly a mere encouragement offered just for Abraham's sake! Indeed, later on, in the book of Exodus, God's ongoing work was affirmed when he appeared to Moses at the fiery bush in Sinai and introduced himself as "the God of Abraham, the God of Isaac, and the God of Jacob" (Exodus 3:6). God took this initiative—the rescue of the Israelites from Egypt—because the offspring of Abraham "cried out" for help and "God remembered His covenant with Abraham, Isaac, and Jacob" (Exodus 2:23-24).

A third reason for taking the blessing promise of Genesis 12:1-3 so seriously is because God affirms it again in the New Testament. Paul, in Galatians 3:8, quotes part of the promise and calls it a precursor to the gospel: "The Scripture, foreseeing that God would justify the Gentiles by faith, preached the gospel beforehand to Abraham, saying, 'All the nations shall be blessed in you.'" Indeed, our justification came by way of Christ's death on the cross, because he became "a curse for us" in order to redeem us—something we'll explore more closely when we look at the theme of biblical trees.

Israel's twelve sons. The means by which we move from Abraham's promise to Jesus is through a set of important individuals and events. In Genesis, for instance, we find that Moses regularly traces faith in the face of sinful autonomy—Adam and Eve's problem in the garden revisited in each new generation—but the subtheme of the blessing-keeper is also carried forward with care. God's arbitrary choice in selecting Abram and Jacob is evident (see Genesis 25, Malachi 1, and Romans 9 about the selection of Jacob instead of his older brother Esau) but some of Jacob's offspring also seem to rule themselves out of the honor of continuing the red ribbon of promise.

We see, for example, the faithless conduct of Jacob's oldest sons in separate stories. Reuben, the oldest, slept immorally with his father's concubine. Simeon and Levi, the next oldest sons, avenged a moral violation of their sister by slaughtering all the men of a village—men who had just expressed devotion to God. These separate reports reemerge in Genesis 49 when, at the end of Jacob's life, he reviewed the character and conduct of each son. Judah, the next son in line after the cluster of Reuben, Simeon, and Levi, was given the status of promise-carrier: "The scepter shall not depart from Judah, nor the ruler's staff from between his feet, until Shiloh comes, and to him shall be the obedience of the peoples" (verse 10).

The pronoun "him" points forward to the coming of Jesus, who, in turn, was able to trace his genealogy to Judah, Jacob, Isaac, and Abraham. The people of his day knew this "proof" was crucial for anyone who claimed to be the Christ.

King David's greater son. The next distinct stage in the progression of the promise appears for us in the stereoscopic stories of King David's attempt to build a temple for God, found in 2 Samuel 7 and 1 Chronicles 17. David knew that the original arrangement given by God in Exodus, in which the ark of the covenant was to be placed in the Tabernacle, and where God's presence on earth would be localized, had long since gone to seed.

At one point during David's career the ark was in the hands of the enemy, the Philistines; and for a long time it was left at a private residence. David eventually brought the ark to Jerusalem, the city which he established as his personal capital for ruling the northern and southern branches of his kingdom (the 12 tribes of Israel had devolved into two inclusive and competing regions in David's era: Israel in the north and Judah in the south). It was time to build a temple to replace the tent in which the ark was kept. Following his custom, David consulted God for his opinion on the matter, asking the prophet Nathan to inquire for him. God refused to let David build the temple; David was too much a warrior to be given that privilege.

David's intention, however, clearly pleased God. David had offered to build a house for God; God, in return, promised to build a house for David. Not a house of stone and timber but a dynastic house—a perpetual kingdom. The rule of this kingdom would begin with Solomon, one of David's immediate sons, but later a greater son would come, one who would ensure that the kingdom would be everlasting. This was an extension of the promise of blessing—a blessing centered on an eternal king of whom God promised, "I will be his father, and he shall be My son" (1 Chronicles 17:13). This son of God offered eternal security not just to David, but to all who would come to know and love David's God. This promise also set up an extension to the genealogical concerns of the Bible: Any figure in history who was to be identified as the Christ—the serpent-slayer—must be a direct offspring of King David.

That trail led to Jesus. The Gospels of Matthew and Luke both trace the genealogy of Jesus in order to demonstrate the correct sequence of Abraham, Judah, Jesse, and David. Jesus is the promise-carrier. Strikingly, within 40 years of Jesus' death, burial, and resurrection, a Roman army destroyed Jerusalem, including all the genealogical records that had been stored there. From that point onward, no one can lay claim to the lineage that is Jesus' alone. The promise of an eternal ruler, seated on David's dynastic throne, was fulfilled in Jesus, a son of David, who affirmed his status as the son of God by his resurrected and eternal life.

2. The Exile and Return

We've mentioned the Babylonian captivity already. It was a 70-year exile during which the Israelite survivors of the Chaldean invasion were carried away to Babylon and elsewhere. At the end of the 70 years a remnant was allowed to return to Jerusalem and reestablish their national identity and the worship of Yahweh at a rebuilt temple. Understanding the exile and return is crucial in tracing the paths of the Old Testament.

Moses introduced the exile theme in Deuteronomy, where he warned the people of Israel that they had a choice: to remain faithful to God, or to follow after the gods of the Canaanites. Moses stated that when the nation arrived in Canaan, under Joshua's leadership, the people were to divide into two groups and recite an antiphonal set of blessings and cursings (see Deuteronomy 27–30). If they remained faithful, Yahweh would bless them; if not, they would be cursed and sent into exile.

Before the exile. The time in Babylon is a dividing point in the Old Testament. Prior to the exile, the people of Israel faced a set of challenges, most of which they failed. The rule of God through judges—a theocracy—was replaced by the rule of kings. After three kings—Saul, David, and Solomon—a civil war divided the nation into northern and southern kingdoms—Israel in the north and Judah in the south. The Old Testament historical narratives describe these two kingdoms as they compete with each other.

Solomon's reign produced a golden age for the united kingdom of Israel and included the building of the temple in Jerusalem. Solomon's reign, however, is presented in the Bible as formative in two directions: in setting up the center for ongoing worship of Yahweh; but also for introducing the worship of alternative deities as he allowed his "treaty-wives" from surrounding nations (that is, wives meant to ensure safe relationships with those nations) to bring the worship of their own gods to Israel. Religious pluralism quickly took root and supported the emerging apostasies from Yahweh, the God of Israel.

When Solomon's son Rehoboam was on the throne, civil war broke out, led by a dissident named Jeroboam. The Bible, from this point onward to the Assyrian and Babylonian captivities, traces comparisons and contrasts between the northern and southern kingdoms. If the reader isn't alert, the many names of the kings who ruled in Samaria and Jerusalem can make the Bible seem like a jumble. The same is true of the various prophets. Isaiah, for instance, offers support to the kings in both the north and the south. By paying close attention, you can begin to see just how real the spiritual, political, economic, and social difficulties of the northern and southern kingdoms are. Israel, through it all, tended to be the most regressive spiritually, with foreign figures such as Jezebel successfully subverting the worship of Yahweh despite momentary reversals, such as Elijah's victory on Mount Carmel.

Eventually, the evil of Israel was so great that God used the great armies of Assyria to invade all of Palestine. Samaria was defeated in 721 B.C. and the northern kingdom of Israel was marched into captivity in a population-exchange program meant to subdue nationalistic instincts. The same Assyrian army that defeated Samaria soon marched against Jerusalem. Hezekiah, the king of Judah, approached God by way of the prophet Isaiah, and pled for supernatural help. It was granted—almost 200,000 Assyrian soldiers died under God's hand, and the attempted invasion failed.

The collapse of the Assyrians offered Judah an additional period of freedom—over 100 years—before another threat loomed from their north: the Chaldeans. The spiritual life of Judah in that period of relative reprieve was filled with ups and downs, but the Bible accounts depict a pattern of increasing apostasy. That led to the Babylonian captivity.

Exile in Babylon. The defeat of Jerusalem by the Chaldeans came in 597 B.C., with some Jews, including Ezekiel and Daniel, being deported to Babylon. The complete destruction came when king Zedekiah, by now a vassal, rebelled. The Chaldeans thus reinvaded in 587 B.C. and completed their devastation. A second deportation followed. Then, in the next century, the Medes and Persians defeated the Chaldeans—prophetically portrayed in Daniel by the "handwriting on the wall"—and the Judean captives were allowed to return home. It all took just 70 years!

Return from the exile. The restoration is recorded in the books of Ezra and Nehemiah. The survivors return to a precarious situation that calls for a bold leadership. Books such as Haggai, Zechariah, and Malachi provide significant insight into the social and spiritual struggles faced by the returned exiles. This became a time for spiritual consolidation in Israel, a transformation that reflects the lessons learned from the period of God's punishment: Idolatry, which was so common before the captivity, came to an end.

Figure 2: A Thematic Overview of the Old Testament

Foundations in **Genesis**:

a. Creation and fall
b. Abraham's blessing

Abraham's offspring, Israel:

a. Organization in **Exodus**
b. Offered holiness in **Leviticus**
c. Transformed in **Numbers**
d. Exhorted in **Deuteronomy**

Israel shifts from theocracy to monarchy:

a. Conquering Canaan in **Joshua**
b. Canaan conquers Israel in **Judges**
c. The promise-carrier is anticipated in **Ruth**
d. **Samuel** finds the promise-king for Israel
    i. Saul is selected but fails
    ii. David, a man after God's own heart

The united kingdom grows & fails (**2 Samuel** and **1 Kings**):

a. Absalom's failed attempt to take David's throne
b. David's son Solomon reigns—the new promise-king
c. Solomon's son Rehoboam reigns—Israel revolts

Judah—the promise-king nation:

When Israel revolts, King Rehoboam is left with the southern half of the former kingdom. A continuous Davidic dynasty is traced through many generations in **Kings** and **Chronicles**. Apostasy grows. Ends with the Babylonian captivity.

Israel—the rebellious nation:

Jeroboam successfully rebels against Rehoboam. He sets up an apostate form of worship. His dynasty is broken. Many others follow in **Kings**. Apostasy grows. Ends wih the Assyrian captivity.

Events of the Babylonian captivity:

God cares for his people during captivity as reported in **Ezekiel**, **Esther**, and **Daniel**.

The prophets:

After Israel divided, God sent a number of prophets to warn and instruct his people. **Isaiah** and **Jeremiah**, in particular, warned about the days of terrible judgment to come. **Ezekiel** and **Daniel** wrote from the captivity, looking forward to restoration. The "minor prophets" help fill in a picture of God's ultimate control.

Judah is restored from captivity:

Judah is no longer independent, but continues to function as a distinct nation. The promise carries forward; events of this restoration are included in **Ezra**, **Nehemiah**, **Haggai**, **Zechariah**, and **Malachi**.

3. The Biblical Trees

A third theme that carries us through the Bible's landscape is introduced by the trees in the garden of Eden. As Sam shared with me in Sechelt, the trees in Genesis and Revelation serve as the bookends of the Bible. The branch growing out of Jesse's root is another element of the theme, which leads up to the main tree of the Bible, the cross of Christ.

The twin trees of Eden. Adam and Eve have a choice to make between the Word of God and the word of the serpent. This theme of choosing or rejecting God's Word sets up a fundamental polarity in life. Should we trust God, or do we trust his archenemy, Satan? Who is *really* telling the truth?

Someone might pause at this point to ask, "Why *this* strange polarity—there are a number of options, aren't there? Namely, the option of trusting our own best judgment, and the judgment of my close friends, and the judgment of sound authorities!" That's the great surprise in this theme—the Bible seems not to recognize any more than the first two options. Another title for this theme might be the "black versus white theme," but the Bible uses trees instead.

The first trees in the Bible are introduced in the context of supporting and satisfying the needs of Adam and Eve: "Every tree which has fruit yielding seed; it shall be food for you" (Genesis 1:29). The role of trees is made more complex, however, when God's creation of a garden for Adam and Eve is described.

> *Out of the ground the LORD God caused to grow*
> *every tree that is pleasing to the sight and good for*
> *food; the tree of life also in the midst of the garden,*
> *and the tree of the knowledge of good and evil.*
> —Genesis 2:9

Adam and Eve were invited by God to eat freely from any and all the trees with one exception: They were not to eat from the tree of the knowledge of good and evil, or they would die. This takes us back to our first theme, of course, as we see how the serpent's invitation to sin, the human response, and God's solution are the platform for all that follows in the Bible. The first theme emphasizes the initiative God took to crush the head of the serpent by means of the promised Christ. The theme of the green trees, by contrast, emphasizes our human role as we respond to God's initiative.

A question that arises about the two unique trees is, "Why this pair of options? Why didn't God offer the tree of life and leave it at that?" It's a question the Bible never answers, but experience suggests the role of freedom in love. For love to be a gift, the one who loves must be free to devote his love elsewhere. God offered such a freedom to Adam and Eve by giving them the option to step away from him—to declare their independence.

As we have seen already, God provided ample knowledge of goodness to the first couple—indeed, everything in the garden had been declared good—but a single tree also offered the knowledge of evil. For Adam and Eve the concepts of sin and death were "empty" categories, something they had never experienced. God offered them that option and, with the serpent's encouragement, they took it. It remains a mystery why they chose to look away from God, or why Satan had done it before them (as we saw before in Ezekiel 28), but it was a possibility, and that possibility became a reality.

The result of their self-focused rebellion was a new self-consciousness: They realized they were naked. Furthermore, God became a frightening figure to them rather than their greatest delight; he was now an overwhelming competitor in the eyes of those who wanted to "be like God."

God met his newfound competitors with grace, covering their shame with the skins of animals who were slain to care for their need. It's at this time that the second tree, the tree of life, comes into special focus. Until God permanently resolved the problem of sin, he was not willing to have Adam and Eve eat of a tree that promised them physical immortality while their souls were dead through spiritual immorality. Thus their access to the tree of life was cut off by sword-bearing cherubs, barring them from the tree of life. They were forced to leave the garden.

The tree of life, as we've noted, reappears once again in the final chapters of the book of Revelation. It is here that the problem of sin is finally and conclusively resolved. The serpent has been defeated and the children of God will once again be gathered into corporate fellowship with him. Rather than rebels, reveling in self-love, the inhabitants of God's eternal kingdom—with Jerusalem as its capital—are now lovers of God. Repentance and regeneration, the gifts of God to his elect, changed their hearts from stone to flesh so that God is no longer seen by them as a competitor but as their Lord and the one who loved them to the point that he sent his son on their behalf.

The branch out of Jesse's stump. The line of Judah, from whom the promise-keeper was to come, was channeled through King David, as we have seen already. Isaiah, however, spoke of the exile theme, promising God's judgment against Israel's flagrant sins. The question for believers in the Old Testament would have been, "What about the promise of the Messiah? How does the exile affect the lineage of Christ?" Isaiah offered an answer: If the twin nations of Israel and Judah are sent off to captivity, the line of Christ will still be protected. This is vividly portrayed in the imagery of a tree that has been cut down, out of which a small branch springs up. From this branch the promise and the people of the promise will be regenerated. The reference point of Isaiah's prophecy is Jesse, David's father:

> *A shoot will spring from the stem of Jesse, and a branch from his roots will bear fruit. And the Spirit of the LORD will rest on him, the spirit of wisdom and of understanding, the spirit of counsel and strength, the spirit of knowledge and the fear of the LORD. And he will delight in the fear of the LORD....He will strike the earth with the rod of His mouth, and with the breath of His lips He will slay the wicked. Also righteousness will be the belt about His loins, and faithfulness the belt around His waist .*
>
> —Isaiah 11:1-4 NIV

The cross. The promise of this branch can only be understood in the context of the main tree of the Bible, the cross on which Jesus was crucified. While the death of Christ would seem, in human wisdom, to mark the end of Christ's ministry, it was actually the culmination of his work on earth. Indeed, the death, burial, and resurrection of Jesus are, collectively, the center point of the Bible's message. The Old Testament anticipated this, while the New Testament unveils it. Through the cross the work of God's merciful reconciliation was accomplished.

Paul, especially, points to the cross in Galatians as the key to understanding God's solution to sin. He presents this in two related themes:

First, the cross serves as a symbol of Christ being cursed for the sake of his redeemed people. Paul cited a passage from Deuteronomy 21:23, which stipulated that the body of any man hung for a capital crime was to be taken down by nightfall. The passage states that a man who was hung was not only guilty before the local community, but also cursed by God. This passage, Paul pointed out, is evidence that Jesus had truly been cursed by the Father. Although Paul doesn't make the point, it is striking that Christ's death came at a unique time in Jewish history: during a period when Israel was under Roman rule and thus used the Roman device for execution, the cross. Jesus, by Jewish tradition, would have been stoned to death and probably not put up on a tree. The cross, as the focal point of all history, set up the final defeat of Satan.

Paul's implicit point is that Jesus needed to qualify for God's curse. He was personally sinless. Thus, only by taking on the sins of others could he be accursed. His death on the cross indicated that God accepted his role in carrying our curse to the cross. From another Old Testament edict, Deuteronomy 27:26, Paul certified this arrangement: Every person who fails to keep every Old Testament Law is cursed. But those who entrust themselves to God in faith are freed from their own curse by Christ's death on their behalf.

> *All who rely on observing the law are under a curse, for it is written: "Cursed is everyone who does not continue to do everything written in the Book of the Law." Clearly no one is justified before God by the law, because, "The righteous will live by faith." The law is not based on faith; on the contrary, "The man who does these things will live by them." Christ redeemed us from the curse of the law by becoming a curse for us, for it is written: "Cursed is everyone who is hung on a tree." He redeemed us in order that the blessing given to Abraham might come to the Gentiles through Christ Jesus, so that by faith we might receive the promise of the Spirit*
> —Galatians 3:10-14 NIV

This exchange makes the function of Christ's death, now symbolized by the cross, the object of faith. Paul explained this to the Colossians using slightly different imagery. The charges held against us because of our sins have been nailed, with Christ, to the cross. Thus we receive the life of Christ in exchange for his taking our death upon himself:

> *When you were dead in your transgressions and the uncircumcision of your flesh, He made you alive together with Him, having forgiven us all our transgressions, having canceled out the certificate of debt consisting of decrees against us and which was hostile to us; and He has taken it out of the way, having nailed it to the cross.*
>
> —Colossians 2:13-14

The second feature in Paul's teaching of the cross is the role it plays as a positive reference point for living by faith. By entering into Christ's death, we find true life. The cross thus becomes an entryway to a transformed lifestyle. The pride that is so much a part of earthly wisdom is now displaced by the humility of the cross. Paul invites us to delight in the new reality: "I have been crucified with Christ: and it is no longer I who live, but Christ lives in me; and the life which I now live in the flesh, I live by faith in the Son of God, who loved me, and delivered Himself up for me" (Galatians 2:20).

The landscape of the Bible, then, is dramatic and sometimes difficult to travel without some good hiking boots. The climb, however, is worthwhile, and it brings us to the foot of the cross, the tree of cursing and forgiveness. From the cross, then, we can look farther down the trail to where the tree of life again waits for us, free for our enjoyment through the rest of eternity.

7

Meeting the Author of the Bible

In March of 1999 I visited London and, much to my surprise, I met the Queen. Upon arriving at London House to check in for a week of research, the receptionist mentioned the local excitement of a pending royal visit. The Queen, as a patron, visits London House about once a decade. So, on the appointed day I returned from the library early to enjoy the event. At the scheduled hour Queen Elizabeth arrived, wearing a red suit amid the splendor of uniformed military officers, suited officials, and elegant ladies. She then led her retinue around the inner courtyard toward the dining room, where a plaque was to be unveiled in her honor. A group of us, wearing blue jeans and sweaters, had gathered along the walkway for a close-up view as she passed by. To our surprise she paused at the beginning of our little line and began to greet each of us in turn, asking where we came from. When my turn came she repeated the question. I told her I was from Portland, Oregon, and was staying in London for just a week.

London House, I should note, is a hall of residence maintained by a private trust for graduate students attending the University of London. The House mainly serves year-round students, but it also has some rooms for short-term former residents like myself. The Queen was surprised: "Oh, just a week?" "Yes," I responded, "and I picked a good one at that!" She smiled and moved on, my ten seconds overwith.

Since then I've reflected both on the significance and the insignificance of the occasion. At one level our meeting was utterly insignificant except as a conversation piece for me. The meeting was a fleeting moment among the many encounters in the Queen's day, and London House was just one of dozens of royal visits in a year—for her, the contact was forgotten as soon as it ended. Even for me, the role of a gawking tourist ended in minutes as I returned to my research.

At another level it was a very significant meeting for me. By human measure, Queen Elizabeth II is a woman of the highest standing—one of the best-known people in the world. I, on the other hand, am a nondescript middle-aged seminary professor. Yet, in the moment of making eye contact with her, and of exchanging brief words, I can now say I've met the Queen. I recognize the empty vanity of the point if that's all there is to it; so let me press on to a larger issue. Speaking *with* her is different than simply knowing *about* her; it was different than an earlier occasion when I had seen her from a distance at Westminster Abbey. In the actual face-to-face meeting I was struck by how much she reminded me of my mother. They're nearly the same age and have about the same stature. The woman who spoke with me, reminding me of my mother, happened to be the Queen of England. My mother, however, offers me much more personal warmth than did the rather restrained Queen. That's not to criticize the appropriate reserve of Queen Elizabeth, of course, but to note that I had enough contact with both women for the comparison to flash in my mind as the encounter ended. In other words, the experience, no matter how brief and limited in substance, still had the unique dimensions and texture of a real relationship.

The lesson of the encounter dawned on me as the Queen continued down the line of residents. The fleeting moment with a mere human, no matter that she was a queen, held no comparison to a much greater acquaintance gained years earlier at Clydehurst Christian Ranch in Montana—my encounter with God himself. I say that not simply because of God's greatness as the creator and sustainer of all that exists, but on a personal level, because God went out of his way to introduce himself to me. He offered himself to me in an act of loving initiative. He even went so far as to reassure me that he cared enough for me to have every hair on my head counted. And since that meeting he has stayed in constant contact with me in the person of his Spirit.

Thus, my relationship with God also has its own dimensions and texture. While such talk may sound overly familiar to you, this is exactly what the Bible constantly offers us. The good news—the gospel—is that the only God, great and mighty, ruler of all that is, has given himself to us to be our God while taking us to be his people. He chose to dwell among us; and, after Christ's ascension, to dwell in us by his Spirit. What's more, he isn't brought down to my level by the encounter; instead, I'm drawn to look up to his infinite stature by the dazzling realization that he cares for me and invites me to know his love which surpasses knowledge. The relationship he brings to us is eternal and life-transforming because he takes us to be his own sons and daughters in Christ. It's much weightier than merely meeting the Queen of England.

What, then, does it mean to know God? While I can speak of the dimensions and texture of relationship with him, he still isn't around for us to see or to talk with as we would speak to each other. Our standard categories of relationship—seeing and greeting each other, eating meals together, and calling each other by phone—don't function with God. Instead—as the skeptic might see it— we speak into the air and call it prayer; we read a book, the Bible, or engage in reflections, and call it listening to God. The fact is, however, that this is a true and living relationship. Furthermore, it defines who we are.

God's Character

If we don't know him, we are, in a very real sense, Godless. However, once we meet him, we discover that his character influences and shapes us just as parental genetics and nurture help define a child. If, in our eyes, God is compassionate and merciful, we will begin to be more compassionate and loving as well. If God is so great to us that he creates a sense of awe, we are certain to be humble of heart. If God is so profound in his wisdom that he causes us to marvel, we are sure to be wise ourselves. If God is so strong as to rule the universe in its every event, then my security will let me sleep deeply at night. As one sage observer put it, "The shape of our character is cast in the mold of our concentration." What, then, are some of the qualities God has that will capture and transform us?

Wisdom

To know God is to meet true wisdom. The Bible discloses a world to us that revolves around God's purposes. So for us to know and respond appropriately to God's greatness is the beginning of wisdom.

Wisdom is the capacity to understand how the world works—the ability to make sound judgments because we increasingly understand the moral and spiritual implications of our choices. We start to see how particular events relate to the whole because we've met the One who designed and sustains the whole. We have a sense of what to pursue and what to ignore; of what to invest in, and what to set aside. With God at the center of the universe, working all things together for good for those who love him and are called according to his purpose (Romans 8:28), we begin to see the futility of trying to climb higher in society by using the bankrupt standards of the world. Instead, we discover true wisdom by seeking God's kingdom and righteousness *first*, while trusting him to support us in the secondary matters of life.

In the language of the financial world, the Bible is a prospectus for eternity. We are invited by God to invest in a partially deferred, long-term, high-yield offer, rather than in junk bonds that promise quick returns but are certain to collapse in the long term. Scripture also discloses the alternative offering: that of the serpent who seduced Eve with the claim that she and Adam could be wise. Indeed, Satan's claim was partly true: He offered to open their eyes to "the knowledge of good"—a knowledge they *already* had by knowing God and enjoying the goodness all around them—"and evil." The final element of his claim is Satan's terrible secret: *His* wisdom is that of the evil "un-world"—the world of the black and white film negative, in which blacks are white and whites are black—the wisdom of death, not of life. He offered wisdom on how to function without the true God. His is a world in which weak, pathetic "un-gods" can be created according to our own whims and used for our own ends. Thus, we truly become "like God" as we create plastic and pliable gods who serve us. Or we discard God altogether.

The serpent also withheld from Eve the cost of autonomy: that functioning without God is to depart from God's life, love, compassion, wisdom, truth, greatness, kindness, beauty, creativity, and glory. Indeed, Satan's offer of evil-wisdom failed to disclose that his promises of apparent freedom actually unleash an enslaving power—through the use of addictive appetites and desires—that enables him to increasingly control his followers, ruling them as their prince (Ephesians 2:1-3).

God, by contrast, offers true wisdom, a wisdom that bears rich benefits now and forever. Satan's realm is the world of darkness and death. We escape it by repentance, by fleeing from darkness to the light; a light that fills us with love, joy, peace, patience, and more—for eternity.

The Bible is explicit when it makes this comparison. In James 3:13-18 we're told of two kinds of wisdom: a wisdom from below, rooted in bitter jealousy and distorted ambition, and a wisdom from above, free from hypocrisy and rich with the qualities of Christ himself. Thus, in meeting God we find an escape from our former wisdom that the Bible calls natural, earthly, disorderly, destructive, and demonic. In its place we embrace the wisdom of peace, purity, mercy, and relational richness.

The conflict between two versions of wisdom was also addressed by Paul, in 1 Corinthians, as he confronted a church nearing spiritual breakdown. What was the problem? Some members of the congregation were elevating their own brilliance and worldly wisdom. They were, after all, children of the great Greek philosophers. Paul, on the other hand (in their view), was an inarticulate, ill-educated, religious huckster by comparison. Paul's message, too, was negative, filled with failure—offering a gospel in which the chief figure died the death of a criminal. Paul's competitors were ready to offer a gospel with greater polish and potential for working in a world of upper-middle class, successful Corinthians.

Paul's response was to agree with the Corinthians. Yes, the wisdom he offered was full of foolishness to the Greeks and based on a reality that made the Jews stumble. But it was *God's* wisdom—a wisdom that clashes overtly with the wisdom of the world. In one wisdom the goal is to succeed by using our own abilities to climb as high as possible. The other wisdom boasts of God's greatness and finds personal pleasure in magnifying others. By meeting God, Paul tells us, we learn of his love for us and are freed from Greek arrogance and Jewish skepticism. Worldly wisdom works only until we die—and then it proves to have been hideously foolish. The other wisdom, by contrast, enables us to begin living comfortably as citizens of heaven even before we arrive.

Heavenly wisdom consists in the fear of God. That is, we embrace the reality that God truly rules his universe, and we begin to reorient our day-to-day choices to that reality. We know that all our rebellious attitudes and actions will be confronted by Christ in the final judgment; and—given our new love for Christ—we find increasing pleasure in the Truth rather than the Lie. Wisdom, then, is the inclination to live in light of eternity, remaining oriented to Christ through life's every moment.

Faith, Hope, and Love

To meet the author of the Bible is to discover meaning in every dimension of life. The measure of healthy spirituality, for the apostle Paul, was summarized in the triad of graces: faith, hope, and love. He wrote to the church in Thessalonica, for instance, that in his prayers he was "constantly bearing in mind your work of faith and labor of love and steadfastness of hope in our Lord Jesus Christ in the presence of our God and Father" (1 Thessalonians 1:3). The best known of Paul's clusters is found in the conclusion of the celebration of love in 1 Corinthians 13, "And now these three remain: faith, hope and love. But the greatest of these is love" (verse 13 NIV).

Each of these three graces reflects the change that comes with meeting God in Christ. He stirs within believers a confidence that was lost in our forefather

Adam. Until we meet God and recognize his care for us, we are faced with the daunting task of taking care of ourselves in a world that more often than not could care less. Faith is the assurance we receive through the testimony of the Spirit in us that God's care for us is even greater than our self-concerns. God now sees us as his beloved children through the work of Christ on the cross. The testimony of the Spirit is a personal work, tailored to us as individuals, but always using the unconditional promises of the Bible. For Abraham, faith came as he entrusted himself to God in the promise that he would receive the long-awaited promise of a child (Genesis 15). This child would be the next link in the chain that eventually led to the promise-keeper, Christ himself.

Indeed, faith always comes by hearing God's word concerning Christ (Romans 10:17), who conquered sin and death. The completed work of Christ in caring for our sins reassures us that there is no work left for us to accomplish. Thus, our souls find relaxation in the certainty of God's love.

As a college student I remember our local InterVarsity Christian Fellowship advisor, Steve Smith, sharing the significance of faith in relationship to hope and love. Faith, he pointed out, has its foundation in the work that God accomplished in the past. The cross is our reference point in faith: Christ died for our sins, once and forever. Faith, in that sense, is my looking back at God's work in history. There, he intervened amid the tragic circumstances of human independence and called us back to a life of dependence: "Abide in me; abide in my Word; abide in my love." We are branches invited back to the vine, who gives us our life. Thus, the past has significance in the present, orienting me to my present life of constant dependence. Apart from Christ's past and present work in my life, I'm unable to do anything except wither.

Hope, Steve suggested, is faith oriented to the future. That is, once we know of Christ's work for us as an accomplished reality, we are given a new status in life—that of God's children. With that standing in mind, we are invited by God to look ahead to the end of history and beyond. The future has a profoundly new significance. Rather than living life within a framework of mere decades, some 80 or 90 years, we begin to see life as eternity and ourselves as citizens of heaven. God's promise to dry every tear and heal every hurt also reassures us as we face our immediate struggles. This hope purifies us, helping us to remain oriented to God's values in a world captivated by human values, because the gaze of our soul is on Jesus, the author and finisher of our faith.

Love, Steve concluded, is the immediate and existential reality of relationship with God. Love is always an event of the present. What credibility, for instance, would a husband's professions of love gain if he promised his wife, "Look, I'll love you next week for two or three days—I've got a project I'm busy with this week so I'm not able to love you until then"? Love has to be something of the present—it may be rooted in the past and faithful to the future—but its place is always in the present moment. Thus, as Steve summarized, faith, hope, and love are located in the three dimensions of time—past, present, and future; but the anchor of all three is our love of God in the present moment. It elevates the present moment without the present moment becoming an idol (as it is to so many people in our existential age).

The role of love in the Christian's life, then, is pivotal. Some teachers describe love as an act of the will—something we chose to do, rather than a compassion emerging from within. Love, defined as will, eventually generates affections, we're told, just as a caboose follows after a train engine. That view seems to have some benefits because it makes us responsible to act rather than to wait for feelings to lead us. But it still represents a Stoic rather than a Christian version of religion. Rather than an act of the self-moved will, biblical love is always a *response* to the one who touches our heart: We love God because he first loved us (1 John 4:19). We then love our neighbor or our enemy because God's love is extended to all that he has created, and we become channels of his spreading goodness. In our response to God's love, we love with our hearts—which then defines our choices through new-found values.

This was a foundational truth of the Protestant Reformation. The church of the late middle ages had adopted Aristotle's premise that we become virtuous by practicing virtues—a spirituality of the will, with a morality applied from the outside-in. Luther, in his *Disputation Against Scholastic Theology* (97 theses posted in 1517, a month or two *before* his more famous *Ninety-five Theses*), denied Aristotle's view, calling it the "worst enemy of grace." Instead, Luther explained, "Having been made righteous, we do righteous deeds"—a morality working from the inside-out. The will, then, always chooses whatever the heart values. Before faith came we were lovers of self and lovers of pleasure (see 2 Timothy 3:1-5). Now we are lovers of God and of those whom he loves—often to our great surprise.

The ground of faith, then, is love. That's the key to our meeting the author of the Bible. He first loved us and gave himself to us in his Son. As Paul puts it in Romans 5:5, the love of God has been "poured out" in our hearts by the coming of the Spirit. Thus, as Paul shares in his own testimony (2 Corinthians 5:14), the love of God compels us to live boldly for him.

Quietness and Glory

Meeting the author of the Bible has a transforming impact—God changes us, as Paul's life illustrated. The encounter, though, isn't what we might expect from an almighty God. That is, the curious non-Christian would probably assume that meeting God must be an overwhelming experience—perhaps something like the Hollywood depiction of Moses in the *Ten Commandments* movie, who returned from his encounter with God with his hair whitened and rearranged into a lofty perm. There certainly is some merit in that notion. The people of Israel, for instance, experienced a rather direct exposure to God when he met with them at Mount Sinai as recorded in Exodus 19–20. There he spoke aloud from the mountain in the midst of fiery smoke, trembling landscape, and enormous sound. The result? The Israelites begged Moses to ask God never to do it again! They were terrified, convinced they would die if it happened a second time.

Nevertheless, that particular event was exceptional. Instead of using thundering drama, God usually discloses himself in a very quiet fashion. A picture of this in the Old Testament is Elijah's meeting with God after he fled from Jezebel to Mount Horeb in the Sinai wilderness:

> *The LORD said, "Go out and stand on the mountain in the presence of the LORD, for the LORD is about to pass by." Then a great and powerful wind tore the mountains apart and shattered the rocks before the LORD, but the LORD was not in the wind. After the wind there was an earthquake, but the LORD was not in the earthquake. After the earthquake came a fire, but the LORD was not in the fire. And after the fire came a gentle whisper.*
>
> —1 Kings 19:11-12 NIV

It was in the gentle whisper that God spoke. It's as if God's general principle of self-disclosure is "quieter is better."

That principle certainly holds true in Christ's ministry. Jesus came as light into the world, but he did so in a subdued fashion. Peter, for instance, was stunned when, just after he correctly declared Jesus to be the Messiah, Jesus began to talk about his coming crucifixion. Peter assumed the Son of God would want to unveil his glory by somehow overcoming the Roman rulers in order to set up his kingdom on earth. James and John, too, both wanted to be part of the grandeur of Christ's coming reign. Instead, Jesus went to the cross silently, like a lamb to the slaughter, while still affirming to Pilate that he was, indeed, the King of the Jews.

With the coming of the Spirit at Pentecost there was a certain amount of drama, but this seems to have had a purpose—it served as God's disclosure of ownership of the church. For the most part, quiet self-disclosure remains the norm in the New Testament. The picture offered by Paul in 2 Corinthians 3:16-18 is especially instructive: meeting Christ is like having a veil lifted.

This passage in 2 Corinthians is profoundly important as a *crux interpretum*—a crucial point of interpretation—for understanding the spiritual life. It jumped off the pages at me during my first Bible read-through on the pebbly shore of Sechelt, British Columbia. I remember how impressed I was with Moses as I read of his direct exposures to God in Exodus 33–34. He was a friend of God, one with whom God had a conversational closeness. He stayed with God for extended periods during Israel's time at Mount Sinai, and was able to have time with God in the tent of meeting. When Moses came away from being with God, the visible glory of God's person remained with Moses such that his face glowed—the first-ever case of fluorescent face. Perhaps any aspirations we might have to be like Moses are too much to hope for, but that unlikely desire was stirred in me as I read about him.

With that still in mind I was amazed, a few weeks later, to reach the point in my reading where Paul told the Corinthians that what Moses had then is *much less* than what God has made available to Christians today! For Moses, God's Word was written and delivered on stone tablets. God kept his distance from Israel—fulfilling their request that he deal with them indirectly through Moses. In the years that followed, it became evident that Israel had failed to grasp a key opportunity—setting up, instead, a man-centered religion.

Moses, at least, had the benefit of being in direct contact with God. But even he began to lose the "glory" of God as he was away from God's manifest presence. Christians, by contrast, now have the constant presence of God, in his Spirit. Paul explains it this way:

> *Now if the ministry that brought death, which was engraved in letters on stone, came with glory, so that the Israelites could not look steadily at the face of Moses because of its glory, fading though it was, will not the ministry of the Spirit be even more glorious? If the ministry that condemns men is glorious, how much more glorious is the ministry that brings righteousness! For what was glorious has no glory now in comparison with the surpassing glory. And if what was fading away came with glory, how much greater is the glory of that which lasts!*
> —2 Corinthians 3:7-11 NIV

Paul then mentioned the veil worn by Moses to describe the spiritual problem of unbelief. Rather than enjoy the shine of Moses' residual glory, the people were distracted by it; so Moses wore a veil until it faded. So, too, the gospel is "veiled" today until a person turns to the Lord in a work of supernatural release from being dominated by "the god of this age." The enemy, Paul explains, blinds the minds of unbelievers to the good news of the glory of Christ "who is the image of God" (2 Corinthians 4:4).

Once the veil is lifted, the glory of God in Christ begins to transform the soul of the unveiled believer. In this process the Spirit of God takes the Word of God to make men and women of God. The Word is essential: It represents the gentle voice of God disclosing truth about himself to the world. The Spirit is the member of the Trinity who applies that truth to our hearts, actually bringing about the change "from glory to glory" in us (see 2 Corinthians 3:18). That is, as we spend time in God's Word, we will grow increasingly "glorious" in our souls, experiencing the work of supernatural transformation.

We won't notice that transformation taking place any more than a child notices that he or she is growing physically in any given day. The change is noticed only when old things no longer fit. For the young teenager their old pants are too short, and their shirts too small. For the believer, old appetites begin to fade and new choices begin to be made in the direction of godliness. The person who expects to "feel" the change, or see it in some dramatic fashion, will be missing the point. The change is a change of heart and values. New behaviors will emerge, but they emerge because of changed desires, so they don't seem foreign. Moses, for instance, wasn't self-conscious about his glowing face; it was those who looked at him that found it strange.

I recall a distinct case of having Christ's glory seen by someone else, while I was unaware of it. I attended Multnomah Bible College from 1966 to 1969. Then I transferred to a local university for two more years to complete my degree requirements. Jim Murray was one of two or three other Multnomah students who did the same, so the group of us enjoyed seeing each other at classes, sometimes eating lunch together, and just hanging out as friends. Those were the days of Black Power—the racial upheavals that rocked Portland and America as a whole.

Our university had a number of activists who were pressing for reforms, sometimes in ways that alienated others. Jim was an African-American. We often talked about the world he experienced as a black man in contrast to my white world—something I needed to hear. But for the most part we enjoyed our deeper identity as fellow believers amid the ocean of non-Christians on the campus.

One afternoon Jim and I were leaving the student commons together when a mutual friend, a woman who wasn't a Christian, called out to us, "Jim...Ron!" We stopped and she came up to us. Without offering any explanation, she said, simply, "I just want you men to know that I really appreciate you. You're both so happy on the inside, it encourages me. I just wanted to tell you." With that she turned around and walked off! Jim and I were Christians and close friends in an alienated world; the glory of the gospel was at work.

Paul also prayed for the eye-opening work of the Spirit in Ephesians 1. There he wrote to the "faithful in Christ Jesus" that he was praying constantly that the "Father of glory" would give them "a spirit of wisdom and of revelation" concerning him. He specified what he meant by using the analogy of vision: "I pray that the eyes of your heart may be enlightened" (verse 18). He wanted them to know three things about God's care for them: "what is the hope of His calling, what are the riches of the glory of His inheritance in the saints, and what is the surpassing greatness of His power toward us who believe" (Ephesians 1:18-19).

Thus, the work of God in lifting the veil of unbelief is both an event and a process. At the beginning we are captured by the remarkable assurance that God has taken us as his own inheritance, dealt with our sins, and loves us. As we grow in faith we need the Spirit to take the Word and reassure us again and again of God's sovereign care for us and of his power to carry us forward to the outcome of his good purposes for us in eternity. Faith, then, is our gaze at Christ as offered in the Old and New Testaments, with the eyes of our heart opened by the ongoing ministry of the Spirit.

The Fruit of the Spirit

In his letter to the Galatians, Paul speaks of the content of God's transforming work in us after we've met him. The fruit of the Spirit is the substance of the character Christ displayed during his ministry on earth. As we gaze at Christ in faith we find that the shape of our own character is cast in the mold of our concentration: We are transformed into his image.

The Galatians, however, had lost their gaze. Paul was upset that they were beginning to look to their own efforts to become righteous after they had met God. Rather than gazing on Jesus, they were focusing upon the behavioral demands of the Old Testament Law. This reversion to a man-centered religion threatened to take the young church backward: "Did you receive the Spirit by the works of the Law, or by hearing with faith?" Paul asked. "Are you so foolish? Having begun by the Spirit, are you now being perfected by the flesh?" (Galatians 3:2-3).

The solution to our continued tendencies to sin is not found in efforts to behave righteously—a transformation from the outside-in—but by the Spirit's work of changing our desires—a transformation from the inside-out. The fruit of the tree displays the type of tree that bears it. Our behaviors need to be changed, of course, but any efforts to change outward activities without having a changed heart will fail—the very error the Pharisees made. Instead, Paul told the Galatians, "walk by the Spirit, and you will not carry out the desire of the flesh" (Galatians 5:16). To be under the Spirit is *not* to be under the Law (verse 18). To walk by the Spirit will transcend the superficiality of the Law, producing "love, joy, peace, patience, kindness, goodness, faithfulness, gentleness, self-control"(verses 22-23)—the kinds of heart-qualities that defy any legal requirement. Indeed, they surpass anything the Law demands.

Indeed, the Lord Is Good

Meeting the author of the Bible, then, is an event and a process. We discover that our seeking him came about only because he first sought us; we find that enjoying him is the fruit of his enjoying his own triune fellowship, which pours outward as a spreading goodness to us; we discover that the love of God changes us in ways that we don't even notice, but others do. Knowing the love of God is the benefit we were made for, and that discovery is the foundation for an eternal wisdom that works here and now. As the Bible tells us in Psalm 34:8—and Art, my early mentor, regularly reminded me—"O taste and see that the LORD is good; how blessed is the man who takes refuge in Him!"

Part II

POWER TOOLS

Section A

Variety Is the Spice of Bible Reading

Some of the men in our college group were out of control. Scott, the Canadian, was waging battle with the Americans in the indoor hot tub. The action raged until water flying out of the tub shorted out an electrical wall plug and plunged that part of the house into darkness. Our college leaders' retreat had been a full day of reading, thinking, talking, and praying. Now, after the hard mental workout, everyone was unleashing their physical steam. We loved it!

Our weekend retreat featured an all-day "Bible Dig-in" loosely modeled after an event I remembered from my own student days with InterVarsity Christian Fellowship. On that occasion, a group of Portland-area college students met in a private home for a day of intense Bible study. It was one of the most productive exercises I'd ever experienced in exploring God's Word. Since then I've used it whenever I have a group ready to grow. Each time, it's been a winner.

The Dig-in is just one of a number of approaches to personal and group Bible studies I've used or seen used.

The read-through approach has rich benefits, as we've seen, but there are many different ways to fulfill Christ's call for us to abide in his Word—any of which are helpful in bringing solid biblical enrichment. In the pages ahead, we'll look at four good options; two are group-centered, offering the benefits of shared involvement in the Bible, and two are more suitable for personal use.

Group Studies

The Bible Dig-In

The Dig-in is an intensive inductive study of a single book of the Bible. I've also heard it called a Manuscript Study because it features the use of a typed, unedited copy of text. The exercise is done as a day-long group event with a number of segments. Each element carries the participants closer to a real understanding of the Bible author's original meaning as he first wrote the text. The goal, by the end of the day, is to have every participant able to talk freely, deeply, and accurately about the message of the selected book. The approach features stronger analytical involvement—work done at very high levels of a person's abilities—than can be found short of a Bible college or seminary course!

The key is that social reinforcements—especially the competitive thrill of the chase—are linked with an obvious and productive sequence of discovery activities. Breaks between each phase allow the students to relax, yet without losing the momentum of the overall effort. By encouraging students to share what they've gained in a low-threat setting, the door opens for them to combine real enjoyment and solid learning. It's a true "bonding experience" both with fellow participants and with God himself.

What, then, makes for a successful Dig-in?

1. *A manageable book or segment.* Not every book in the Bible invites this approach. Genesis or Romans, for instance, are much too long. This approach lends itself, instead, to books between one and six chapters long. Many of the New Testament epistles by Paul, Peter, or John are good candidates. In the Old Testament the minor prophets are also good prospects, although some might be a bit cryptic. Ruth and Malachi are excellent options. A self-contained segment from a larger book can also be selected, such as the Sermon on the Mount in Matthew 5–7, or the Upper Room Discourse of John 13–17. The key is to pursue a section that will provide a clear sense of success and benefit in the time allowed.

2. *A motivated group.* Not everyone is hungry for what the Bible offers. Just as with the read-through, the people to invite are those who already show interest in personal growth and serious Bible study. It is certainly fair, however, for ministry leaders to make the opportunity available to everyone in a group, but they *must* be clear about what's coming: intensive Bible study! Pity the poor student who comes to this event when he's really expecting a chance to hang out with friends for a weekend while enduring a few religious talks. If ever there is a place for "truth in religious advertising," this is it. A leader can, of course, promise very high returns for those ready to take on the challenge. The first experience of the Dig-in by a group will make it a high-reputation event for subsequent occasions.

The size of the group may vary from small to large, but I'd recommend a minimum of eight so that the participants can break up into teams. There is a clear social dimension in a Dig-in that prospers when a collection of creative personalities have been stimulated by a challenge. The participants will enjoy themselves and each other, so bring as many to it as possible. The upper limit is a function of space and the leader's leadership skills—20 or 30 (or more) is fine. The various exercises are done within subdivided groups, so a sense of small community can still be present even in the context of a large community.

3. *A comfortable setting.* A Dig-in works well in homes with large living rooms or with adjacent dining, kitchen, and den settings. The warmth of a home offers a great learning environment, and the ability to deploy and regather the subdivided groups to a common room is key to this approach. My high-school and college groups have done well sitting on carpeted floors. Adult groups would probably prefer chairs. The goal will be to use the home throughout the day, including the lunch break and the sharing time at the end of the day. A retreat center can work as well, of course, but the Dig-in lends itself to being a day retreat for which a home is a great option.

4. *A typed, non-paragraphed copy of the Bible text.* The substance of the Dig-in is an inductive study. Inductive work always begins with the raw data and searches for inherent structures and order. The editors of our Bibles have done much of the work of identifying the units of thought by forming paragraphs (which aren't present in the original Hebrew or Greek texts). The Dig-in returns that task to the students. The various editions of the Bible, we should note, often disagree on where paragraph breaks belong, so it really is an important exercise to think about such units.

The manuscript should each be line numbered for the sake of common reference by the group. Here is an example of the restructured text of Ephesians 1:1-7, using the rather literal NASB translation. When you prepare the text, leave enough space between the lines for underlining and small notations:

Ephesians (NASB)

1. Paul, an apostle of Christ Jesus by the will of God, to the

2. saints who are at

3. Ephesus, and who are faithful in Christ Jesus: Grace to

4. you and peace from

5. God our Father and the Lord Jesus Christ. Blessed be the

6. God and Father

7. of our Lord Jesus Christ, who has blessed us with every

8. spiritual blessing in

9. the heavenly places in Christ, just as He chose us in Him

10. before the foundation

11. of the world, that we should be holy and blameless before

12. him. In love He

13. predestined us to adoption as sons through Jesus Christ

14. to Himself, according

15. to the kind intention of His will, to the praise of the

16. glory of His grace, which

17. He freely bestowed on us in the Beloved. In Him we

18. have redemption through

19. His blood, the forgiveness of our trespasses, according

20. to the riches of His grace.

The manuscript should continue in this format to the
end of the book. Offer wide margins for note-taking and
page numbers, and have each new page of the manuscript
text lines begin with a "1" (to avoid unwieldy numbers near

the end of the book). Thus a student can report an observation item as found on "page 3, line 12," or simply "3-12".

5. *An agenda of activities.* The activities of the day form three repeated cycles of observing, reporting, and resting. The second and third cycles build on the results of the prior stage as each captures more of the book's complexity until the book's overall theme is identified.

For the activities, the group is broken into teams. For the sake of explanation, let's assume we have 19 people in our group. We decide to form three teams—Red, White, and Blue. Two teams have six students, and one has seven. These teams will report their discoveries during the report phases. For the first observation scan in each cycle, the teams subdivide even more, this time into pairs or threesomes. Let's name these pairings the Firs, Pines, and Oaks.

Cycle 1: *Finding repeated words, phrases, or concepts.* The goal is to work as fast as possible, without being concerned about catching everything. The teams can choose their own strategy for doing this. As we look at Ephesians, for example, the goal is to find any important repetitions that tell us about Paul's themes or emphases. The Firs, Pines, and Oaks in team Blue might want to subdivide the manuscript pages—with the Firs looking at pages 1 and 2, the Pines at 2 and 3, and the Oaks at 3 and 4. Team Red might let everyone loose on the whole manuscript in order to see connections in the whole that might otherwise be overlooked. Team White might have fast readers do the whole book (placing the two fastest readers in group Oak) while groups Fir and Pine split coverage of the four-page manuscript so each group reads just two pages.

This phase lasts just 30 minutes—about long enough for an average reader to get through the entire book. The students may complain that they are being rushed, but that's part of the dynamic!

Each participant should have a notebook in which to write their observations. Encourage the participants to look for the most meaningful words they can find—the idea is to discover Paul's main themes. Clusters of words or ideas are very important (such as Paul's use of "to the praise of the glory of His grace" which is repeated in varying forms in Ephesians 1:6,12, and 14).

At the end of the first 30 minutes, the Tree groups regather into their Color teams, and then are given an additional 20 minutes to come up with the most important and most numerous repetitions they've discovered. A team reporter needs to be designated for the report time that follows. The overall leader should remind the teams to look for quality, not just quantity, of repetitions. For instance, in Ephesians the phrase "holy and blameless" is repeated just twice (1:4 and 5:27), but it offers a great insight into God's purpose for his church.

The Color teams are then called together to the main room and asked to report what they've found. This should take 20 minutes. The ministry leader leads this session. A good way to keep things moving is to give the Color teams a set of opportunities to report in round-robin fashion. That is, each team gets to name five of their top repetitions. A large dry-erase for recording the findings will help keep track of the items reported and reinforce the amount of content gained in less than an hour of searching! In the meantime, the leader should begin to transition from merely recording the reports to asking for more general comments on what was learned in the process. For example, were there any outstanding surprises or discoveries?

At the end of this cycle it will be time for a 20-minute break. The participants are likely to be "up" at this stage, ready to socialize (and some will want to talk personally about what they discovered). The break time will seem too short; make sure to keep things moving at this stage!

Cycle 2: *Finding paragraphs.* The second cycle focuses on determining the paragraph breaks in the manuscript. A paragraph is a key building block in constructing ideas. It contains a primary idea, usually reinforced by a set of supporting ideas. The goal of this exercise is to identify natural paragraphs—noticing the seams between new elements in the Bible content. In this segment the participants follow the same sequence and time frames as before. When the Tree groups reconvene with their Color teams, each group should offer reasons for their key decisions. Some decisions will have been harder to make than others; the hard ones invite the most attention. Note, too, the divisions that were the most distinct (for instance Paul's introduction should be easily distinguished and might serve as a preliminary example of what the members should look for). They often represent the major elements of the book.

By the end of this cycle the group will be more than ready for a hearty lunch break, followed by the third and final cycle.

Cycle 3: *Finding the author's purpose and main structure.* In this segment the groups should follow the same sequence as before, but the observation phase should include more time for the Color teams to meet and less for the Tree groups. This is the hardest exercise of the day because more difficult judgments are called for than before. Each of the Color teams should come to the final all-group session ready to offer a purpose statement and an outline (for instance, "Paul's central purpose in writing Ephesians was.... Evidence for this is found in three major themes, namely: 1...2...3...").

The schedule for the day might look like this:

9:00-9:30 Welcome and light breakfast items

9:30-10:00 Orientation and team selections

10:00-11:10 Cycle 1: *Finding Repeated Words, Phrases, and Concepts*

> 10:00-10:30 Small groups (Fir, Pine, Oak), observations
>
> 10:30-10:50 Team meetings (Red, White, Blue) to form a report
>
> 10:50-11:10 Joint session for Color team reports; discussion

11:10-11:30 Break

11:30-12:40 Cycle 2: *Finding Paragraphs*

> 11:30-12:00 Small groups (Fir, Pine, Oak), observations
>
> 12:00-12:20 Team meetings (Red, White, Blue) to form a report
>
> 12:20-12:40 Joint session for Color team reports; discussion

12:40-2:00 Lunch break

2:00-3:10 Cycle 3: *Finding the Author's Purpose and Main Structure*

> 2:00-2:20 Small groups (Fir, Pine, Oak), observations
>
> 2:20-2:50 Team meetings (Red, White, Blue) to form a report
>
> 2:50-3:10 Joint session for Color team reports; discussion

3:10-3:30 Break

3:30-4:30 Report and application: What did we discover today?

The Open Forum

A second group-centered Bible study is the Open Forum; or, as I first ran into it, the "Rap Session" (a title some might not want to use on account of the term "Rap music"). As much as the Dig-in is an inductive exercise, the Open Forum is deductive: In it, a single topic is used to guide a review of the Bible as a whole to discover what God has to say about that topic.

My discovery of the Open Forum study format was indirect. I was invited by Bill, my roommate from Bible college days, to speak at his winter high-school camp. Bill had been a youth pastor at a church in Boise, Idaho for a number of years already, but this was my first chance to see him in action. I was teaching the college-age group at a church in Spokane at the time, so I lowered my normal content level when I came to the first session of Bill's retreat. His 60 or so young people were energetic—in fact, a bit too rowdy for comfort. But when I stood to speak, they were with me all the way. I soon realized that my content was too low for them; so I kept raising it until it was well beyond what my Spokane college class could handle. Bill recruited me soon after that to lead the college ministry at the church. I was happy to join him, in part to see what drove this remarkable ministry. The Open Forum study method was a key part of the ministry's success.

The genius of the Open Forum is its function of engaging a person's questions with applicable biblical content while also building skills in Bible study. This student-centered approach relies on the questions of real life to produce its benefits and increases the students' investment in learning.

The Forum is a single discussion with four embedded movements. Given the slow pace of open dialogue in addressing content, the Forum functions best if it runs for at least an hour; I prefer using an hour and 15 minutes.

First is the Question Identification exercise; second is the Opinion Phase; third is the Bible Discovery Phase; and fourth is the Summary exercise. The leader guides the first and fourth functions, while the students are primary in the second and third. The leader is a facilitator throughout the exercise.

Certain rules are necessary. The foremost are: "Thou shalt say nothing critical of another person's opinion," and "God's Word must be taken seriously no matter how foreign it seems at first." Over the years I've used the Forum as one of my favorite growth tools. Chris, for instance, was a skeptical college student who asked the most difficult—and best—questions. He was captivated by the Bible content offered through the Forum. Here's how it works:

1. *The Question Identification.* The question always comes from the participants. Group members are usually shy about asking hard questions when the Forum is first introduced. Part of this, I suspect, is that it's so counter-cultural! That is, because churches usually feature teacher-centered forms of education, it's a bit strange to be invited to ask honest and potentially threatening questions.

The first few weeks of using this approach, then, tend to attract old chestnuts such as, "Does the Bible teach eternal security?" or "Can God make a stone too big for him to lift?" Fair enough; but the group really gets productive when participants start asking questions closer to their hearts than their heads. To get launched, I invite them to think through the various categories of life: What are the challenges they are facing in their relationships with their parents, siblings, friends, or romantic interests, as well as with God? What are they struggling with at work? What questions do they have about ethics, science,

Bible doctrines, or anything else they might be thinking about or struggling with?

In time, the members begin to save questions they think about during the week, and bring them to the Open Forum. These questions are usually more applied and personal: "My mother and I had a big fight—she seems to want to control my life; so what does it mean for me to honor my mother now that I'm 23?" Or, "I found out that the guy I always work out with at the health center is gay, so now I want to avoid being anywhere near him. But that's not what I should do as a Christian, is it?" Life is God's best training center, but for it to be productive, we need to learn how to engage the questions of life with the truths of the Bible.

The Forum leader needs to honor every question—even one careless remark or casual dismissal of a question will have an immediate chilling effect on the group. Nevertheless, the leader's role is to make sure a question has as much applicability as possible. The example given above about the woman who had a fight with her mother was a real one. I asked her if it was all right if we broadened it a bit and asked, instead, "What does it mean for us as adults to honor our parents, whether it's an awkward relationship or not?" She happily agreed, and in the course of the discussion she had her particular concerns addressed, but not as the exclusive topic of the evening.

As I've promoted the Forum ministry over the years, a common concern leaders have is the number of questions that should be addressed in an evening. My answer is that only one question should be entertained in a session. Furthermore, I always honor the first hand raised—once the question is called for, it becomes the question for the night. This teaches participants that every honest question is important. In time, the participants learn, too, that every question "works" because the fabric of life has threads that run in every direction—no matter where the fabric is pulled, a number of additional issues are woven into it. A single question is also best because it takes reflective time in a dialogue to sort out values, fears, and foggy thoughts. If, on the other hand, a number of questions are addressed in one evening, either the leader ends up becoming the "Bible Answer Man," or the questions are answered too superficially to make the time as useful as it could be. The secret is to allow the members of the group to do the work, and time needs to be allowed for that.

2. *The Opinion Phase.* In the opinion stage, all the participants are invited to express their personal views and feelings about the question. This should be allotted between 15 to 20 minutes. The rule here is that everyone is welcome to hold a view—and their views are not open to criticism. This is important not only to ensure a sense of security for participants, but also to discover the spectrum of opinions on the subject. If someone feels strongly about the issues raised, he or she is welcome to express his or her feelings as long as it's done responsibly and without demeaning others. The leader should make it clear that any use of Bible content here is premature. That comes next.

The views offered in this phase are often controversial, so why invite them? Because it promotes honesty and allows freedom to discover the level of insight already present in the group. It also forces group members who haven't been concerned about the particular issue to see some of the complexities that are present. Finally, it gives freedom for participants who aren't committed to Christian values a chance to express themselves—and to gain some ownership in the exercise. There's a secondary benefit, too—namely, an application of the symmetry principle. If everyone gets a chance to express themselves freely, then God has a similar right to have a voice once the Bible phase is reached.

A practical matter about leading the discussion should be noted. In any group discussion, certain personalities prosper. Thus, the leader needs to guard against dominating the group himself or allowing any cluster of the more verbal members to dominate. A good way to handle this is to announce regularly that every comment must be brief and succinct; and that no comment can include multiple points. Call it the 20-second rule—anything that needs more time than 20 seconds needs to wait for a subsequent 20-second exposure. This has to be addressed when the Forum is first introduced and reiterated at the beginning of every subsequent session. The leader can, of course, make his own judgment about when and with whom the rule is applied (that is, some members may take a minute or so to make a point but everyone *wants* to hear it). The key is that everyone has a chance to express themselves and to be treated fairly.

It's best, too, to have the seating arranged in a circle. Group dynamics are influenced by the physical space in which they occur. For a group discussion to work, everyone needs to have a clear line of sight with whomever is speaking. Rows or even a semicircle cause the group to focus on the person in the front.

3. *The Bible Discovery Phase.* Here is where the best action occurs. Some readers may be wondering at this point how a Forum can be considered a group Bible study. Try it and find out! Be sure that everyone has a Bible in hand—a few "house" copies need to be available for those who forget to bring theirs or simply don't own a Bible. Coach the students to bring their own Bibles—this will help them to become more familiar with the key sections of the Scriptures.

At first the participants' involvement in this exercise may be a bit weak, but their skills in applying biblical content will begin to emerge as the Forum becomes a standard feature in the ministry program. It complements the use of other Bible-study exercises—the read-through especially—by offering an applied situation where various Bible passages can come into play. Earlier, I wrote about Way's transformation as he began his first read-through. It was in the Forums that it became apparent to the group that something unusual was going on in Way's life—indeed, he was the person who, though once very quiet, now had to be reeled in by the 20-second rule from time to time! He was alive with passages that applied to the question at hand because he was saturated with content from his Bible reading.

To put the benefit differently, our discussions about God's point of view on important issues made it glaringly evident that some folks didn't know much about the Bible. However, in time they began to come on board by joining the exercise of thumbing through pages of text trying to find a passage they vaguely remembered. It helps, too, to have an unabridged Bible concordance in the room for those who want to refer to it. For those who don't know the Bible well, but find the Forums helpful, the motivation for more serious Bible reading and study will begin to grow.

The Bible discovery phase is the time when the more knowledgeable members get to prosper because they generally bring a broader Bible knowledge to the discussion. Their knowledge becomes a resource others can draw from. In the course of a Forum, for instance, someone will volunteer a key passage relating to the question. That offers the leader a chance to invite everyone else in the group to turn to that passage to see for themselves what it says and how it applies. On occasion the leader can prime the pump by suggesting a resource himself: "Doesn't it say something about that in 1 Corinthians 13? Anyone want to check that out?"

Sometimes in the Forum discussions, participants will give cliché responses (for instance: "Well, God tells us to pray about it," or "We need to let go and let God work!"). When this happens, a leader needs to press the group for more. That may call for responses like, "Does everyone understand what Steve just said? Can someone please explain it for us?" Playing ignorant is useful to keep things moving.

At times a student may say something that is perfectly clear and biblically accurate but he or she seems tentative while speaking. Rather than support them, I may take on the "devil's advocate" role and challenge them by acting as if I hold to an unorthodox alternative (especially if I know that alternative can be found in the secular community). That forces them to argue their case more strongly by marshaling more evidence; and it invites others in the group to pitch in further support. It also sharpens individuals for the occasions when they really do meet someone at school or work who holds the position I've adopted for the moment.

4. *The Summary Phase.* During the last five or six minutes of the Open Forum, the leader needs to take back full initiative and offer a summary and conclusion. This includes reinforcing the key points made during the evening while still pointing to some areas where the members need to do some further reading and thinking. It's an opportunity to motivate by praising the members for the work they invested in the exercise, and to encourage them to underline the sections of the Bible that were most important in addressing the question. This brief segment is important because it serves as the final memory of the evening activity—so the sharper the focus, the stronger the sense of benefit they carry away. Depending on the nature of the question for the evening, it can also be a time when the leader and one or two others pray for the person who raised the question.

Personal Bible Studies

Tracing Bible Themes in a Book

One essential key to growing a sound theology—an accurate view of God and his ways—is to be careful with key definitions. During my Army days in Washington, D.C. I had time to explore a growing curiosity about the different ways the Bible is interpreted. I was leading a newly formed singles ministry at Barcroft Bible Church and would offer what I thought was a common point of view, taken from my days at Bible college. Some in the group insisted otherwise. At the time I was also attending a Christian Reformed Bible study where I discovered different views from my own on a number of issues. Then, near the end of my tour, I had a chance to do a six-week internship with *Christianity Today* magazine, which exposed me to still wider views among evangelical Christians. A book published since then, entitled *Five Views of Sanctification* (and others like it), would have been a real help to me in those days!

A solution was to take my Bible to see what Paul, for one, had to say about such things. The great benefit of this semi-inductive approach (that is, we start with a term to probe the content; but we let the content itself guide us from that point onward) is that we build good study skills in exploring our primary source, the Bible. I started in Romans. The exercise proved to be one of my most productive personal Bible studies ever. While it requires solid effort, the benefits make it worthwhile. I commend it with four stars!

1. *Begin with a concordance.* I was aware of the triad of graces—faith, hope, and love—that Paul often points to in his works, including the most well-known, 1 Corinthians 13:13: "But now abide faith, hope, love, these three; but the greatest of these is love." I took these, then, as crucial

foundations for any Christian theology and decided to trace Paul's use of each word in Romans, a book known for its theological substance. I started with "faith," worked on it for a week, then moved to another word the next week, and so on. After the triad of graces I looked at "grace" itself, then concluded with "glory." I made five trips through Romans in five weeks, following a new term each time through. In the process I also traced the way Paul used "flesh," "death," "life," "law," and so on, because these words were intertwined with my target words.

My initial guide for each trip was a comprehensive (unabridged) concordance. My goal was to trace every use of the word and any cognate forms of it ("faith," for instance, is directly linked to "believe" in the Greek text: *pistos* and *pisteuo*). I took advantage of my Bible college studies in Greek and used the *Englishman's Greek Concordance* to find every use of the underlying Greek word, even if it was translated differently in my English Bible (as, perhaps, "confidence"). With every use of the selected word identified, I began my survey. A concordance is a treasure for this approach. For the readers who don't read Greek, there are ways to get the same benefits in an English-only concordance. See the discussion on concordances on pages 167-70 for a summary of how this works.

2. *Explore each context.* At first I highlighted each use of the selected word in my Bible. Then I read through Romans at one sitting to see how the word functioned in the flow of the entire letter. I was curious, for instance, to see what other words were linked to my target word—faith and grace, for instance, were tied together in Romans 4. Also, did Paul include the word (in this case, "love") in any oft-used phrases such as the "love of God"?

All these exposures helped orient me to the way the word was used in Scripture.

The next step was to look at the immediate context to analyze how the selected word is used in that setting. Is it a guiding concept? Does it depend on other related terms? Is the word repeated a number of times in the context? What is the overall point of the paragraph in which it's used? How does the word work within that paragraph? If I were to build a definition of the word based on the way it's used in this paragraph, what would be its key feature? How does the paragraph in which the word is used contribute to the next larger context (perhaps the chapter as a whole)? Does it form a theme in the book as a whole? These aren't magic questions, but they worked for me. The secret of an inductive pursuit is to keep asking what the writer had in mind when he wrote the passage and used the word.

3. *Write a definition.* The final stage of my survey was to write a definition of Paul's use of the term in Romans. Until we engage in writing it's easy to float above our content. The definition forces us to make decisions: What is the core concept (if there is one) that ties together every use of the term? What are the variations from the core concept? Faith, for instance, might have a core concept of "absolute reliance" while it might have variations in separate contexts such as "reliance on God associated with salvation," or, separately, "reliance on human capacities." A good definition will list the core element and, following that, all the variations—with a list of the verses that best support each.

The strength of tracing Bible themes is that we end up much closer to God's theological definitions rather than settling for traditional assumptions. Any particular insight also remains anchored to the whole. That is, a given verse must be viewed as part of a whole, and the book must be accurately grasped for us to be confident about our particular point. The tradition of making theological assertions, buttressed by prooftexts, is useful only if the prooftexts are all true to their original contexts. Adopting that kind of accuracy is a crucial responsibility. If the Bible student addresses a text without remaining fully aligned to the intention of the original author, then the authority of the student's teaching is really his own. Instead, God's authority, located in the biblical writer's authorial intention, must be our focus.

Multiple Readings of a Single Book

Several years ago I spent a year serving as an admissions representative for my Bible college. For my road trips I obtained library tapes of well-known speakers to help while away the hours on the highway. One sermon, out of dozens, reached out and grabbed me. It's not that I remember the sermon, but I remember the way in which the minister prepared himself for the sermon. Or, more accurately, the way he prepared for his sermon series. He decided to preach on a certain book, with the series to begin just over a month later. Then to prepare himself he began reading his target book all the way through for each day of the intervening month. By the time he began his specific preparation for the first sermon of the series he had just completed his thirtieth reading of the book! That's something Sam or Jack would have done, and I adopted the approach for myself, even though I'm not a pastor with ongoing sermon responsibilities.

The day came, however, when a church near Bremerton, Washington, asked me to serve as their interim pastor. I agreed to the arrangement and, for my sermon series, selected the book of Ephesians. I began reading through Ephesians once each day and continued for a month. It was a pleasure!

The benefit of repeated readings within a relatively brief period of time is obviously in the familiarity it produces. By the end of the month, a reader can think his way through the book and offer a rather accurate paraphrase. Certain features, such as Paul's deep confidence in Christ's care for him, start to emerge as major profiles in the book. It's not that Paul ever says, "Christ likes me," but it's obvious that Paul is convinced of it. Such an insight would likely be missed if a person were to read the book through just three or four times in a lifetime, or if a pastor read Ephesians only one paragraph at a time in preparation for his sermons on that book.

The beauty of the multiple-reading model is, like that of the read-through, its simplicity. It bears high dividends by making the reader alert to the writer's tone and nuances, while not calling for any complex exercises. It also treats the book as a complete literary unit—which is what we would hope for if someone were to read a letter we sent them. That's the way the New Testament epistles, especially, are meant to be read.

Section B

Resources for Bible Reading

Throughout this book we have promoted a very direct approach to Bible reading: Start fast, and don't slow down! But it's also important to be able to follow up questions that will arise in the course of reading your Bible. A broad range of resources are available to support you in this pursuit. Some of the resources, like a concordance or a topical Bible, will be useful for tracing specific themes or words in the Bible. Other tools explain where the Bible came from and how it was transmitted. All invite serious attention from serious students.

Bible Translations

Modern Bible translations offer readers excellent options for serious Bible reading. However, there are differences among them that we should understand. In some circles there will be concerns about the underlying text from which the translation is made. Another matter to consider is the translator's strategy in converting the language of the original text into English. Finally, the question of what belongs in the Bible—the canon—needs to be addressed.

The Original Text

The original Bible books were written in Hebrew (with a few sections in Aramaic) and Greek. These materials were copied by hand and widely distributed. Thousands of very old fragments and complete texts have been identified, with the Dead Sea Scrolls predating even the time of Christ. Some early translations of the Bible (from places like Babylon and Egypt), are also useful to scholars for comparison with the Hebrew and Greek texts. Thus, translators can work with a wide selection of sources, especially when translating the New Testament.

Through the ages, when old copies of Bibles were worn out, new copies replaced them. This process of transmission inevitably led to variations in the content—some of the copyists were less disciplined than others in reproducing the text. Sometimes the changes were intentional as a copyist attempted to smooth out difficult passages; sometimes a change was the result of simple carelessness. The result is that modern translators have a vast number of early texts available to consult as they do their work— especially when it comes to the New Testament. The variations are mostly modest and have no substantial bearing on the content. What's more, many Bibles display these minor differences in the marginal (or center-column) notations that also contain cross references.

An example found in both the New American Standard Bible (NASB) and the New International Version (NIV) is Romans 8:28, where both versions adopt the reading that *God* works for good in everything, rather than adopting an alternative text used in the New King James Version (NKJV) that "all things work together for good." In one Greek text God's role is explicit, while in the other it remains implicit.

Sometimes the differences are more significant, but never enough to threaten a biblical doctrine. An example of a passage that may not belong in the New Testament but is still doctrinally reliable is the story of the woman caught in adultery (John 7:53–8:11). Because it is not found in most Greek texts of John, this segment is placed in brackets by both the NASB and the NIV. The story may well have been a genuine event in the life of Christ, shared among early Christians, but it was probably inserted in John's Gospel only after the Gospel was completed. Still, the central point of this story—Christ's display of mercy—is supported elsewhere (see, for instance, the forgiveness granted in Luke 7:36-50). A second trouble spot is the ending of Mark's Gospel. These two sections aside, nothing threatens our confidence that the content of today's Bible is essentially what the original documents offered.

The question of how we received our present Bibles is a matter better left to Bible Introductions (see page 172), but the question of textual transmission and reliability has a bearing on how some of our modern English versions are to be distinguished from each other, so some very preliminary comments are in order .

Some translators rely on the specific textual "family" of New Testament documents compiled by the sixteenth-century Christian humanist, Desiderius Erasmus. Families of texts are groups of Bible manuscripts that share unique features. These unique aspects—a set of distinctive phrasings—point back either to an early copyist from which the subsequent distribution of texts emerged, or to the original phrasings of the first writers themselves, from which all other manuscripts strayed.

The textual tradition gathered by Erasmus came to be called the *Textus Receptus*, or Received Text. The 1611 King James Version (KJV) was based on this text. A revised version of the Received Text (which addresses some conspicuous problems in the original work by Erasmus) is now called the Majority Text by its proponents. The title comes from the fact that its textual family represents the numerical majority of extant Bible manuscripts. With this in its favor (and buttressed by some more technical arguments), proponents of the Majority Text view that tradition as the touchstone of textual orthodoxy. The Bible translation that relies on this tradition—the New King James Version—adopted the title of the earlier KJV in order to underline the continuity of the *Textus Receptus* tradition while setting aside the archaic English of the original version.

Those who reject the claims of the Majority Text proponents use a different method to identify as accurately as possible the original words of the Bible. They argue that simply counting the number of extant manuscripts in a tradition is to confuse quantity with quality. They also note that the majority of the texts cited by the Majority Text are relatively modern, rather than the older (albeit fewer) sources preferred in their tradition. Instead, the proponents of this eclectic alternative to the *Textus Receptus* recognize a number of textual families and draw from among them—assuming variations of strength and weakness—in order to build as reliable a text as possible. Two of the texts they favor are the oldest known complete manuscripts—*Codex Sinaiticus* and *Codex Vaticanus*—which were not available to Erasmus. They are works of exceptional quality, presumably the labor of very careful copyists.

Proponents of the eclectic text also work with a set of assumptions about how errors are likely to accumulate, and evaluate texts on that basis. They argue, for instance, that scribes were more likely to modify a verse to make it easier to understand, than vice versa; thus the more "difficult" a verse, the more likely it is to be the original rendering. This textual approach is the more widely accepted of the two among modern scholars, and the Greek texts that come from this eclectic tradition stand behind most of the Bible translations on the market today.

Having reviewed these matters, we need to return to our earlier point: The content of all the Bibles we have today is profoundly reliable—none of the differences being debated by the textual scholars threaten any doctrinal concerns. The key truths of the Bible are so broadly based that occasional textual disputes don't affect them. Thus, any translation will be productive for use in a Bible read-through.

Approaches to Translation

When a Bible translator in some subtropical region translates Isaiah 1:18, should he translate it to say that our sins will be made "as white as snow," or "as white as pure milk"? This question is important because many such tribes have never had any exposure to snow, and their languages have no word for it. Wouldn't Isaiah's point be more effectively transmitted to the tribal audience by the analogy of milk? Or is it better to give them a new word— "snow"—and then inform them of its meaning at a future time?

Such questions stand behind a pair of approaches to translation. One of these, the *dynamic equivalence model*— best represented by the NIV—seeks to transmit the ideas of the writer so that the impact received by the reader will be very similar to that received by the original readers. The second approach—represented by the NASB and the NKJV, among others—is the traditional *word-for-word correspondence model*, which holds that words represent meanings within a context. The task of the translator is to find, in the receptor language, a word as close as possible to the word of the original language. By correlating those words as consistently as possible, the reader is able to recognize shifts in meaning or nuance through the context.

What are the differences in practice? The reader has less work to do in the dynamic equivalence model and is able to read with greater freedom and flow; but the reader in the word-correspondence model has the benefit of being better informed by making more of the judgments required in cases of complex meaning. An example of this is found in Romans 5–8, where the NIV regularly translates the Greek word *sarx* as "sinful nature." *Sarx* literally denotes the soft tissues and muscles of a body, or more broadly, the corporal nature of a person—thus the NASB consistently translates it as "flesh." The dynamic equivalence approach helps the reader see that Paul consistently links *sarx* with sinful attitudes and behaviors throughout this section of Romans. Thus it helps readers by more fully interpreting the word for them.

The trade-off, however, is that the NIV reader will certainly miss the important link Paul makes between sin and the physical body. A digression is in order here before I move on: Paul, in Romans 5–8, makes repeated references to "flesh" and "members" in relation to the body. Sin and death, he teaches, still reside in our bodies despite salvation (see Romans 7:24–8:2)—that is, in our flesh; and the problem with our present bodies won't be resolved until we receive resurrected bodies (Romans 8:23). Paul links sin to the body in a way that suggests a pollution of our attitudes and activities. The pollution is a deeply embedded habit of sinning—the dark side of the physical habits that also help us accomplish daily behaviors without careful thought (such as shifting gears in a car while viewing scenery, or eating while we read). So, in this case and many others, the careful Bible student will prefer the freedom to reflect on issues as offered by the less interpretive NASB.

How do other translations fit into this polarity of approaches? Of the major translations in publication today, the NIV is the primary representative of the dynamic equivalence approach. A close cousin would be the New Living

Translation that follows after The Living Bible (LB). The original Living Bible, published in 1971, was a rather free paraphrase of the Bible, initially meant for children. Its surprisingly strong acceptance by adults paved the way for dynamic equivalency and the NIV (1978). However, The Living Bible maintained a place in the market along with the NIV despite being technically flawed by its informal roots. The New Living Translation is a major revision by professional translators who were careful to retain the biblical text's accuracy while still keeping the lively style of The Living Bible.

The more literal word-for-word correspondence versions are aligned with the venerable old King James Version, which still retains popularity in some circles today. At the turn of the twentieth century, translators took advantage of new textual materials that had surfaced and offered new translations in the KJV tradition with the English Revised Version (1881) and the American Standard Version (1901). Neither of these were particularly successful. The Revised Standard Version (1952) was a successful effort to update the still-clumsy style and language of the ASV. The New English Bible (1970)—more oriented to England's tastes—offered similar benefits. Some conservative Christians were concerned by the affiliation of the RSV with translators and institutions they viewed as liberal; thus some conservative evangelicals launched another major American translation, the NASB (1971). It was widely welcomed despite a rather awkward style that is a nearly word-for-word translation of the underlying Greek text. The NASB also retained archaic pronouns ("Thy," "Thee," and "Thou") in any references to God, as well as the odd KJV convention of beginning every verse as a new paragraph. These clumsy features and the awkward style opened the market door for the much more readable NIV. The NASB-Updated Edition (1995) has removed the archaic pronouns, and some editions offer a normal paragraph format.

The Roman Catholic Jerusalem Bible (1966) should also be noted as a fine translation. It broke a Catholic tradition of using the Latin Vulgate Bible as the underlying text for translations, and adopted the Semitic and Greek texts instead.

Any one of these recent Bible translations will serve well for Bible read-throughs (as will other careful translations that continue to emerge). I've personally enjoyed using the RSV (and look forward to trying the New RSV), the NIV, and the NEV on read-throughs, even though I generally stay with the NASB because I prefer it for teaching purposes. I happily and quickly adopted the updated edition of the NASB when it became available.

The Canon

Roman Catholic Bibles, and Bible versions meant for both Protestant and Catholic readers (the NEV and the RSV) all include the books of the Apocrypha, located between the Old and New Testaments. Why are they there? And how should they be treated in a read-through by those whose Bibles contain them?

This brings us to the issue of the Christian canon. The *canon* is the official list of books recognized by the church as those God intended to be part of the Bible. The books of the Old Testament were joined by an additional set of books in some editions of the *Septuagint*, which is the Greek version of the Old Testament. These additional books number 14 or 15 (depending on lists and on how books are linked to other books) and most of them were written in the two centuries before Christ's birth. Their contents vary, including prophetic works, instructional manuals, legendary pieces, and historical books. First Maccabees, for instance, is a very useful history of the

Jewish wars during the intertestamental years. Despite their usefulness, they were not included by the Jews in their canon of sacred books, nor did Jesus identify them when he spoke of authoritative works. Thus, they were used by Christians through the centuries, but were treated with serious reservations. Jerome, for instance, the translator of the Latin Vulgate Bible, rejected their canonicity.

The issue became controversial with the coming of the Reformation. When Martin Luther translated the Bible into German, he set the Apocrypha apart and introduced them as useful works, but not God's words. Soon after that, at the Council of Trent, the Roman Catholic church determined the opposite, declaring the majority of the books to be canonical. That was the first official recognition of the Apocrypha by any formal church body.

In the Protestant tradition, I concur with Luther and the other reformers. Nevertheless, the Apocrypha would be useful to read on occasion, and 1 Maccabees is an especially important work for explaining the circumstances of Israel during the New Testament era. I don't, of course, include the Apocrypha in my read-throughs.

Bible Atlases

Short of spending a year touring Israel and the Middle East, nothing will bring the Bible to life better than a good Bible atlas. The Bible reader should, at the very least, select a Bible with a good set of maps included as an appendix, and then refer to them regularly during the course of a read-through. Readers are quickly awakened to the scale of some of the events of the Bible by looking at the distances involved—as in the case of Joshua's "longest day" (Joshua 10). We are given a sense of who Elijah is, including his remarkable physical endurance, once we look at the distance he traveled by foot after defeating the prophets of Baal on Mount Carmel. We then discover the depth of his concern when, the next day, he began a trek of more than 100 miles south to Beersheba, and then on even farther to Sinai, to escape Jezebel's threats against him (1 Kings 18–19).

However, as useful as the maps in the back of our Bibles might be, they dim in comparison to the benefits of a serious Bible atlas. A good atlas will include pictures of most of the important landscape features in Israel, topographical maps that show the terrain, maps that trace the important travel routes, and vegetation and rainfall maps that reveal, for instance, striking differences between the relatively lush Galilee and the arid regions of Hebron and Jericho.

A good atlas will also offer detailed discussions of key biblical events and corresponding maps to illustrate the movements of the people involved. Typically you'll find that the maps are arranged in chronological order, so the events of the Old Testament are traced first, followed by the travels of Christ in the New Testament, and then the missionary travels chronicled in Acts and the epistles. Some atlases also review archaeological discoveries and discuss their application to the Bible.

An excellent atlas—of coffee-table quality—is the *Holman Bible Atlas*, which includes many color plates of Bible lands, as well as excellent maps, text, and charts. Herbert May's *Oxford Bible Atlas* is a solid work that offers all the basics.

Thomas Nelson Publishers offers two very practical tools that invite special notice. *Nelson's 3-D Bible Mapbook* by Simon Jenkins offers a collection of computer-generated maps featuring quarter-angle elevated views of the Bible landscape—views that produce a 3-D effect when you look at the topography. With arrows to indicate movements, he traces key Bible events in a uniquely effective manner. A second resource is *Nelson's Complete Book of Bible Maps & Charts,* which offers useful charts, maps, and teaching aids that the publishers permit to be copied for use in Bible studies.

Resources for Examining Bible Words, Themes, and History

One of the great benefits of Bible reading is that we begin to discover the specific characteristics of God—"his ways," in biblical parlance. Some of these—his love, grace, truth, mercy, and many more qualities—invite readers to trace them as themes. The Bible also confronts readers with unknown people and places. The Assyrians and Chaldeans, for instance, were primary nations used by God to confront his people. They were also major players in world history. Men like Herod and Pilate, who lived in the time of Jesus, are known to historians apart from the Bible. Resources are available that offer a comprehensive historical context for Bible narratives.

Concordances

A concordance offers an alphabetical listing of important words used in a book, along with references for finding the locations where the word was used. If, for instance, someone wants to trace the number of times Tychicus (one of Paul's traveling companions and letter-carriers) is mentioned, and what the circumstances are for each occasion, a quick trip to an exhaustive concordance is in order. There we find that he's mentioned five separate times, each in a different book of the Bible. Citations under the heading of Tychicus would include the location in the text and a brief section of the text itself. The first entry, for instance, is, "Acts 20:4 and from Asia Tychicus and

Trophimus 3034." The listing might simply offer a "T" in place of Tychicus in order to keep the cited text brief.

The number at the end of the entry ("3034") is an additional tool found in all the major concordances. It refers to a dictionary entry offered elsewhere in the concordance, where the Hebrew, Greek, or Aramaic root word is listed and defined. The word will also be shown in the original language (Τυχικός, for instance, is the original Greek rendering for Tychicus) and a transliteration (*Tuchikos*). This feature is especially helpful when a number of different words in the original languages underlie the English word. The English word *love* for instance, has a number of different Hebrew and Greek words behind it (for instance, in Hebrew, *'ahav* and *chashaq*; in Greek, *agape* and *phileo*).

Not all concordances are created equal. Many Bibles include partial concordances as an appendix. These are most helpful in alerting a person to some useful verses on a given topic, but are usually too limited to help the reader find a particular verse on the basis of one or two remembered words in the verse. For such occasions a Bible reader needs to have a comprehensive concordance.

We've referred to an *exhaustive* concordance already. It's a comprehensive concordance. That is, it includes every word found in a given English translation of the Bible, even down to the conjunctions and articles. *Strong's Exhaustive Concordance of the Bible*—or an updated edition, *The New Strong's Exhaustive Concordance of the Bible*—offers format improvements and some additional study tools, using the King James Version as its referent. *Strong's* dictionary numbers (like the 3034 in our example earlier) are used by other Bible study tools so students can cross-reference those tools with the Bible texts and the dictionary features of the concordance. Exhaustive concordances are also available for other versions of the Bible, including the NIV and the

NASB. Readers should adopt the concordance linked to their preferred translation of the Bible, if possible.

Another pair of concordances—well known to seminary-trained Bible students—are George V. Wigram's *The Englishman's Hebrew Concordance of the Old Testament* and *The Englishman's Greek Concordance of the New Testament.* These are just what their titles suggest—concordances of the original Hebrew and Greek words, but with the text portion of the target word offered in English rather than in the original language. Thus, while our friend Tychicus would be listed under Τυχικός rather than under the anglicized and transliterated form of his name, we would still find the segments of verses for all five uses of his name—and the verses are in English.

The great advantage of using the *Englishman's* concordances is that every use of the underlying Hebrew or Greek words is included in the verse listings, no matter how the English versions might translate them. Thus every use of *agape*, or "love," can be identified and separated from the "love" based on *phileo.* And, conversely, a certain word that might have two or three ways of being translated, such as the Greek word *sarx,* which has been translated as "flesh" or "sinful nature," can be examined comprehensively because every use is listed under the Greek heading, no matter what the English translation might be. Among other things, this quickly shows a student the range of meanings that can be found in the original word.

The disadvantage of using the *Englishman's* concordances, of course, is that readers need to know how to read the Hebrew and Greek text of the concordance headings. One solution is to learn to read the original alphabets, a task accomplished on the first day of seminary courses for each of the biblical languages. More realistically, another solution is available: *Strong's* dictionary numbers are linked to recent editions of the *Englishman's* concordances. Thus a student can take number 3034 from *Strong's* concordance, go to the *Englishman's* concordance, and find the Greek entry he's looking for by using the number. The numbers from *Strong's* are also cross-referenced with a separate set of numbers in *The NIV Exhaustive Concordance*, so the latter tool can also accomplish the same purpose. It's an exercise well worth the effort.

Topical Bibles and Bible Dictionaries

One useful tool found in many Bibles is cross-reference verses placed in the margins. For example, if you read Deuteronomy 6:4-5—"Hear, O Israel! The LORD is our God, the LORD is one! And you shall love the LORD your God with all your heart and with all your soul and with all your might"—and then look at the cross-references in the margin, you'll notice that Matthew 22:37 and Mark 12:29 are cited. That's because these are places where Jesus quoted the words from Deuteronomy 6:4-5.

Orville J. Nave took the concept of cross-referencing a step further. In *Nave's Topical Bible*, he compiled more than 20,000 topics and collected related verses under those headings from throughout the Bible. Each verse is quoted in full, which allows the reader to compare the related content from the entire Bible. Because Nave's work was completed when the King James Version of the Bible was the primary English translation for Protestants, the verse selections are from that version. Recently another edition of Nave's, keyed to the NIV, has been offered: the *NIV Nave's Topical Bible*. This edition is also linked to the *NIV Exhaustive Concordance* word numbering system, which allows the reader to check on every use of a particular word if he or she wishes to take the additional step.

A cross between a topical Bible and a Bible dictionary is *Vine's Complete Expository Dictionary*. This resource combines W. E. Vine's work, which addresses the New

Testament, with a later effort by Merrill Unger and William White, which covers the Old Testament.

Bible Dictionaries

Bible dictionaries are single-volume resources offering brief encyclopedia-like essays on most of the major people, places, and events in the Bible. They offer historical information—including details about archaeological discoveries—that can enrich our reading of many biblical narratives. A pair of older but useful works are the *Wycliffe Bible Dictionary* and *Zondervan's Pictorial Bible Dictionary*. A more recent effort, very well done, is the *Holman Bible Dictionary*.

Bible Encyclopedias

The Bible dictionaries have much larger, multivolume cousins—the Bible encyclopedias. These resources are similar to general encyclopedias, but their concerns are strictly biblical. Any significant people, places, events, concepts, or doctrines are addressed in solidly researched articles. The articles are often illustrated, and provide ample information for serious Bible students. The major works in this category are *The Zondervan Pictorial Encyclopedia of the Bible* and the *International Standard Bible Encyclopedia*. The latter work is somewhat weightier in its academic concerns, but either set will do much to satisfy the general curiosity of eager Bible students.

Bible Introductions

Bible introductions explain what we know of the origin and transmission of the various parts of the Bible. As a young student I was fascinated with F. F. Bruce's *The Books and the Parchments* as well as his *History of the Bible in English* and *New Testament Documents*. Using works by Bruce and others, I burrowed into additional studies and archaeological resources to discover all I could about such matters, and shared that information with my students. Any Bible student should buy at least one of these works to read and keep as a reference source when questions arise. To that end, Bruce's works are still useful. So, too, is Norman L. Geisler and W. E. Nix's *A General Introduction to the Bible* and David Ewart's *From Ancient Tablets to Modern Translations*.

Section C

The Bible Books in Summary

In the pages ahead, we are going to walk through brief introductory summaries for each book of the Bible. You'll recall that in chapter seven, we reviewed the landscape of the Bible. Some of the themes of chapter seven will be reflected in the summaries to follow, but they won't be developed at length. If you would like an even more developed introduction to the books of the Bible, tools are available at most local Christian bookstores, ranging from Old Testament and New Testament Introductions, to individual commentaries for each book.

The Old Testament

Genesis is the seedbed of all key Christian truths, including (to name just a few) creation, revelation, sin, salvation, and how to grow in faith. It begins with the creation of the universe, including humanity on the earth. The problem of sin and its solution are paramount in the book. The promise God gives in 3:15 to resolve sin— crushing the serpent's head—is traced through the book by the set of cryptic blessings which affirm that through Abram's family all the nations of the earth will be blessed.

This is first offered in 12:1-3. From that point onward the book is focused on Abram and his offspring, with particular attention given to displays of increasing faith in the lives of the key figures—this despite their inevitably daunting circumstances.

The book is also structured by a regularly repeated colophon, "this is the account of . . ." (or "these are the generations of"—the Hebrew word is *toledoth*), which separates the prior narrative from a narrower discussion that follows. For instance, in Genesis 1 the subject is God's broader work of creation. In 2:4 it narrows to the particular creation of Adam and Eve within the context of the garden of Eden. Thus while the creation of Adam and Eve in chapter 2 repeats an element of chapter 1, Moses' purpose is clear: "I want you readers to focus on only *one* aspect of what I just introduced." Other examples of these *toledoth* breaks can be seen in 5:1, 6:9, 10:1, 11:27, and so on. Once again, these features accentuate the importance of the pivotal individuals in the overall narrative.

Exodus summarizes the development of Israel as God's chosen nation, a nation meant to present God to the rest of the world. Its begins over 400 years after Genesis ends. Moses, the central figure, is God's man called to rescue Israel from the Egyptians, who had subjugated Israel as a labor force. The book has two phases: First, the exodus of Israel from Egypt, for which the book is named. Second, the agreements made between God and Israel, which included the Ten Commandments; a host of additional moral requirements; details about the duties and dress of the priesthood; and instructions about the construction and furnishings of the Tabernacle where God would live among the people. The book includes the first rumble of coming problems when, while Moses is away, the people violate their new covenant with God by building a golden calf meant to represent Yahweh. This, needless to say, doesn't go over well with God. The book ends with God's fiery appearance, which inaugurates the use of the newly constructed Tabernacle and its furniture.

Leviticus teaches us about God's holiness. It draws boundaries and demands righteous behaviors. It prescribes sacrificial ceremonies to express devotion to God, to address individual sins, and as ongoing exercises of atonement for the nation as a whole. The book of Exodus explains the ways in which Israel was to relate to God. Such worship, however, is now foreign to those of us who aren't used to seeing animals slaughtered and who tend to see sin as mistakes or dysfunctional behavior. Against such notions Leviticus sets out one of the most important issues of the entire Bible: namely, that God demands blood, representing death, to be shed in payment for our sin. That frightening reality anticipates the eventual sacrifice of Jesus, whose shed blood is God's solution for sin to all who believe in him.

Along with this crucial content, the book offers a blend of ceremonial, civic, and behavioral regulations. Be sure to observe the importance of personal and corporate holiness in the book as well as the principles of an atoning sacrifice. In fact, the New Testament book of Hebrews should always be read in conjunction with Leviticus, as the former shows how Jesus satisfied the requirements given in Leviticus. Leviticus also contains sparkling passages, such as the call for readers to love their neighbors as they love themselves (Leviticus 19:18), which Jesus identifies as the second greatest commandment (see Mark 12:31).

Numbers is about the transformation of Israel over a 40-year period. The nation is numbered twice in the book, with each census listing separate generations. The first census, in chapter one, represents the generation of men who grew up in Egypt; the second census, in chapter 26, numbers their sons. Each occasion is a mustering of soldiers, listing all the Israelites "twenty years old and upward, whoever is able to go out to war" (Numbers 1:3). The military goal is to conquer the land of Canaan, their promised homeland. But the trip through the Sinai desert required time for receiving and assimilating the covenantal rules and roles we discover in Exodus and Leviticus. During this time the first generation, despite their initial relief at being out of Egypt, found the difficulties of wilderness life to be less than attractive. They responded with grumbling and moments of rebellion. Moses was their immediate target, but their underlying unhappiness was with God, whose presence is conspicuous among them, displayed by a fiery cloud hovering over the Tabernacle. God responds by meeting their needs and by confronting their rebellion— many are killed in a variety of judgments. An expedition of spies, sent to scout Canaan for the anticipated invasion, is the turning point of the book. Only two of the 12 men sent on the mission expressed confidence that God would help Israel to successfully conquer the land. The people followed the ten pessimists rather than the faithful two. As a result, God refused to allow that generation to enter the land. The book then traces the 40-year period of transition from the faithless parents to the emergence of more faithful children—a transformation by testing.

Deuteronomy is the farewell sermon of Moses, which reflects contractual overtones: If the people respond to God's word their future will be prosperous; if they rebel, they will face misery and eventually be thrown out of the promised land that lies before them. Moses reassures them that God will remain faithful even if they, or their distant offspring, should fail: a future captivity would be followed by a restoration. The key elements of Deuteronomy are Moses' restatement of the Ten Commandments in chapter

5 and his summary in chapter 6 of the underlying motive that shapes the desired obedience: The people are called to love God with every dimension of their being—heart, soul, and might. This call to love God wholeheartedly is a refrain that carries through the balance of the book and into the historical books that follow. Kings will be measured by their devotion to God, a God who is rich with lovingkindness and jealous for the affections of his people. The book ends with the death of Moses and a transition of leadership to Joshua, his long-term assistant.

Joshua was called upon to lead the people in their invasion of Canaan. His book reflects the relative faithfulness of the second generation (of those who escaped from Egypt) in contrast to their less faithful parents. The main features of this fast-paced book are its battle accounts—with two major campaigns, one in the region of Jerusalem and the other reaching far to the north, beyond the Sea of Galilee—and the allocation of the newly conquered lands to the tribal clans. The book sparkles with an underlying theme of faith: some people display it (including Joshua—most of the time—and Rahab, a prostitute in Jericho) while others don't (Achan, for one, whose theft of some items devoted to God was linked to a rare military defeat for Israel).

Judges summarizes the mostly dismal record of the third, fourth, and following generations from the exodus out of Egypt. If the first generation proved to be consistently contentious (in Numbers), and the second consistently faithful and bold (in Joshua), then the third generation and their offspring showed that both types of parental heritage were still to be found. Various leaders—the judges of Israel—emerged among the newly decentralized tribal groups after Joshua's death. The book traces crisis after crisis as it becomes evident that Israel's faithfulness in worshiping God was becoming an increasingly rare quality; instead, everyone "did what was right in his own eyes" (Judges 17:6) and trouble ensued. In each crisis, God intervened by raising up new judges who, while proving to be effective in confronting intrusive neighboring nations, also reflected the declining character of the nation as it drifted in its spiritual and moral autonomy. Despite such downbeat assessments, the narrative in Judges is exceptionally brisk, including memorable stories such as Deborah's role in defeating Sisera, Gideon's use of fleeces to make decisions, and Samson's philandering escapades.

Ruth is a short, romantic story placed in the era of the judges, and serves as a wonderful reminder that God is in the business of transforming lives. It begins with Naomi, an Israelite wife and mother who traveled to Moab with her family in order to survive a famine in their homeland. In Moab her husband and two sons died, leaving her with two widowed Moabite daughters-in-law. One of them, Ruth, escorted Naomi back home to Bethlehem—a potential problem, since to the Israelites, Moabites were outcasts. Ruth was instrumental in God's work of turning Naomi from bitterness to joy through Ruth's marriage to a relative, Boaz, who accepted the role of a "kinsman redeemer." The book draws readers back to the red ribbon of God's promise by explaining that King David is the great-grandson of Obed, a child born to Boaz and Ruth.

1 & 2 Samuel—originally a single composition, both books present the transition from the era of the judges to the dynasty of King David, from theocracy to monarchy. Three men dominate the narrative: Samuel, Saul, and David. Samuel and David were both men with a profound devotion to God; Saul, by contrast, was unstable emotionally and spiritually. The first movement of 1 Samuel is the story of Samuel's rise to prominence amid the collapse of the decaying leadership then being provided by the high priest's clan. As Samuel grew older and his able leadership of Israel neared its end, a grassroots movement in favor of a monarchy developed. God responded by directing Samuel to anoint a king in the mold desired by the people— namely, Saul, a man who was physically imposing and, at times, offered bold leadership. His flaws, however, were many and continued to unfold to the day of his death. David was selected to replace Saul but many years go by before the transition occurs. Much of 1 Samuel tells the story of the difficulties between Saul and David.

Second Samuel begins with the emergence of David's rule after Saul's death. One of David's chief priorities was to build a national capital in Jerusalem and to institute the worship of Yahweh in the city. He brought the ark of the covenant to the city and then proposed building a temple to house the ark and to replace the Tabernacle as a worship center. At this point God denied David's request but, in a remarkable response, extended the promise to David that his greater son would be the eternal ruler of an everlasting dynasty. From this high point the book turns to the destructive consequences of David's immorality with Bathsheba.

1 & 2 Kings—at first a single book, both trace the Davidic dynasty through his anointed son, Solomon, then his son Rehoboam and the many Davidic kings who followed. The division of the united kingdom, led by Jeroboam during Rehoboam's reign, produced a rebellious counterpart to the Davidic kingdom of Judah. This northern kingdom, Israel, was less loyal to Yahweh. Major prophets such as Elijah, then Elisha, were active in confronting the apostasy of both nations, but Israel in particular. More supernatural events are clustered in these writings than are found anywhere else in the Bible, save the time of Christ's ministry. The kings are all graded by the author, with many condemned who "did evil in the sight of Yahweh" and a few who did what was "right in the eyes of Yahweh." In time the northern kingdom, Israel, was defeated, with most of the survivors being carried away by the Assyrians to distant lands. Second Kings ends with Babylon's defeat and forced exile of the Judeans as Jerusalem is burned to rubble.

1 & 2 Chronicles is another paired work divided, like Kings, at the transition from David's rule to Solomon's. It complements the other sources that cover this era in that the author is concerned more with matters of community order than with personal matters. David's infamous sin with Bathsheba and his family scandals, for instance, don't draw any notice. But family connections (in genealogies) and the importance of the ark of the covenant, the Tabernacle, and the newly built temple are all carefully reported. So, too, are the spiritual and political welfare of David, his family dynasty, and the southern kingdom, Judah; more so than the parallel discussion in Kings. The writer, it seems, is concerned with the proper worship and honor of God. The selective genealogies that introduce 1 Chronicles carry the reader from the days of creation along the red ribbon of crucial Old Testament families, even to the listing of gatekeepers in Jerusalem. Anyone associated with God and his city are important! The books end with Judah's return from captivity in Babylon—which raises the prospect that Ezra, or one of his fellow-workers, was the author.

Ezra and *Nehemiah*—connected works that may have been part of Chronicles at one time, both describe aspects of the return of the Judean captives to their homeland. While Ezra focuses on the reconstruction of the Temple, Nehemiah is concerned with providing regional security by rebuilding the collapsed walls of Jerusalem. Both books display the strength of individual leaders in the face of a hostile and tenuous setting. Regional political figures in Israel, which is now a province of the Persians, are not ready to see the Jews reorganize their worship and their government. God ordains that both goals are providentially supported by two Mesopotamian kings, Cyrus and Darius, and through the astute work of Ezra, Nehemiah, and their companions. Sin emerged once again in Israel as many community leaders entered into idolatrous mixed marriages with local women. The issue was met head-on as Ezra, for one, reminded his people that just such a sin stood behind the disastrous exile in Babylon. The community responded by ending the illicit marriages. This marks a turning point in Bible history; from here onward the problem of overt idolatry among the Jews is no more. God's discipline has made its impression.

Esther celebrates God's providential care for his people. It is placed in the Persian capital of Susa during the rule of King Xerxes. The Jewish protagonists, Mordecai and his adopted younger cousin Esther, are pitted against the vain Persian antagonist, Haman. Esther is elevated to be queen and Mordecai a high official, but this comes in the midst of a near-disaster for the Jewish inhabitants of Persia. This brief story, rich with irony, never mentions God, but God's providence is a silent context for all that occurs. This is a book to read in one sitting.

Job offers a hard look at suffering and God's use of evil for his own purposes. The book is a summary, written in an ancient poetic form, of a cyclic debate between Job and three men, with a fourth speaker added near the end. It begins with a prologue that discloses Satan as a provocateur whom God stirs to engage the righteous Job (which Satan does by bringing about a set of disasters); it ends with God addressing Job directly. Job's three "friends" in the debate all shared the premise that suffering is necessarily a reward for sin—therefore, given Job's terrible disasters, Job had to have been a terrible sinner. The reader knows from the prologue that this isn't the case; and Job knew it too, based on his godly life. Nevertheless the friends, rotating in their speeches (with each cycle offering harsher assessments), imposed their assumption on Job, insisting that he confess his secret sins. Job, after proclaiming his innocence to the friends, turned his frustration heavenward and insisted that God, to be fair, should disclose his (Job's) righteousness. The fourth speaker charged Job with error for his insistence that God was accountable to justify Job. God then spoke, affirming the fourth speaker's point, and called Job to a proper humility. God then restored Job's fortunes.

Psalms is a collection of diverse poetic reflections about God, many written by King David. The Hebrew poetry in this book offers a symmetry of ideas through its regular use of parallelism; that is, a first line is followed by one or more additional lines that repeat, enhance, compare, or contrast with the first line. A given Psalm may offer an emotional outburst, a question, a complaint, or an extended expression of thanksgiving. Some of the psalms anticipate the coming Christ.

Proverbs offers another expression of Hebrew wisdom poetry. Most of the proverbs are focused on human conduct rather than on God's character or works. A proverb typically consists of two to four lines expressing a pithy moral observation. As in the Psalms, Hebrew parallelism is used, with contrasts made regularly between wise and foolish conduct. Some proverbs contradict others (occasionally within a single parallelism), showing that many of them are meant to be applied only in specific contexts. Many of these striking thoughts would do well to be placed around a home or office on placards as regular reminders of practical wisdom.

Ecclesiastes expresses Solomon's search for significance and satisfaction. He explored the main categories of stimulation, including the pursuit of wisdom, pleasure, materialism, labor for its own sake, prominence, and power. In every test he found that the pursuit leads only to vanity. Wisdom, he concluded, is rooted in God; and happiness is a gift given by God. The book, then, probes life with a realistic cynicism but retains a fundamental devotion to God.

Song of Songs is an erotic love song. It represents the development of a romantic love between a man—perhaps Solomon—and a dynamic young woman. Varied voices carry the song forward, including those of the two lovers and a chorus. The mood swings from exhilaration, to despair, to delight as the relationship experiences moments of separation and restoration. Early Jewish readers linked this song to the messianic Psalm 45 and concluded that the love song prefigured Israel's relationship with the coming Messiah. Some Christians, including Bernard of Clairvaux in the middle ages, adopted this approach but see the king as Christ and the bride as the church. However it is read, the Song celebrates the richness of human intimacy.

Isaiah—the first of the major prophets, which include Jeremiah and Ezekiel, all of whom deal with the culmination of Judah and Jerusalem's faithlessness toward God. Isaiah is notable for its striking prophecies about the coming Christ, with passages from chapters 7, 9, and 53 widely cited in churches during the Christmas season. If viewed in its historical setting, Isaiah traces Israel's defeat by the Assyrians, and Judah's miraculous escape. If viewed as an anticipation of the coming promise-king, the Messiah, Isaiah presents both the reigning Messiah who will rule the nations and the suffering Messiah who will die for the sins of others.

The structure of the book is broadly chronological. Chapters 1–35 deal with the Assyrian threat, including oracles or prophecies about various regional nations. These collected warnings will seem disjointed to first-time readers. To appreciate this, imagine your response if God offered specific warnings about his plans for the near future of Russia, Great Britain, Germany, France, and the United States. Interest in such prophecies would be acute, especially if you live in one of those nations! Chapters 36–39 repeat the events found in 2 Kings 18–20, focusing on King Hezekiah and Judah's providential survival of Assyria's invasion. Chapters 40–66 anticipate the coming of the Babylonian invasion and God's sovereign supervision of these events. Within this section are statements about Israel portrayed as God's servant-nation and God's plan to work through the coming Messiah, the preeminent servant. Read Isaiah with an eye for God's delight in the faithful obedience of his people and his toughness toward those who pay only lip service to him.

Jeremiah offers a revealing picture of the difficulties felt by the prophet as he offers an unwelcome message of coming judgment to an arrogant nation. Judah, having survived the earlier invasion by the Assyrians, concluded that God's temple in Jerusalem was a divine good-luck charm. They were certain they would be safe from similar invasions, even while they engaged in promiscuous worship of other gods. Jeremiah is, like Isaiah, a collection of prophetic summaries and warnings from God. Much of the time the content is carried forward without clear transitions; nevertheless, the book has a basic chronology. It traces 1) Jeremiah's warnings of God's impending judgment as well as the first and second Chaldean invasions and sieges of Jerusalem; 2) a brief reprieve from the second siege (when Jeremiah is arrested); 3) the renewed siege; 4) the collapse of Jerusalem; and 5) Jeremiah's involvement with the survivors who are not taken to Babylon. Jeremiah, unlike the other prophets, included personal elements that offer poignant moments, such as the discovery that the citizens of his hometown, Anathoth, were plotting to kill him. He expressed his unhappiness to God on a number of occasions and God answered him with firmness leavened by compassion. The book portrays the confused status of truth in a fallen society where loyalty to God is seen as sedition and faithfulness to God is rewarded with imprisonment and the threat of death.

Lamentations, traditionally attributed to Jeremiah, is a postscript to the book of Jeremiah. It offers the same personal pathos evident in the prior book, lamenting the sin of Judah and the demise of her capital, Jerusalem, while remembering God's mercy. The author speaks honestly, wrestling with God's terrible judgment, which allowed for Israel's pagan enemies to rule the rubble of God's house. This outcome makes God seem like an enemy rather than a friend. The author, however, finds consolation in the certainty that eventually, God's great love and compassion will prevail and Israel's enemies will face their own judgment for their harsh treatment of God's people.

Ezekiel—this prophet wrote of Judah's last days while he was already in Babylon as a captive. The decline of Jerusalem came in stages, with an early surrender of the city to the Chaldean forces. Zedekiah was made a vassal-king over Judah by the Chaldeans, but eventually he rebelled. This led to the final capture and destruction of the city, as reported by Jeremiah. Captives such as Ezekiel followed events in Jerusalem from afar; many of them assumed Jerusalem would regain independence. Ezekiel told them otherwise: Jerusalem was doomed because of her history of apostasy. Ezekiel is among the most dramatic of the prophets, using imagery that startles and stirs. A vision of God's glory amid a collection of creatures and wheels within wheels introduces the book. Another vision is of a valley of dried bones that come together as resurrected bodies. Like the other prophets, Ezekiel was cryptic and suggestive (rather than comprehensive) as he displayed the depth of Judah's antagonism toward God, along with her neighbors, and the consequences of their rebellion. As you read Ezekiel, look for the prophet's development of themes such as glory and God's name (that is, his character): Yahweh is insistent that Judah will know that he is God! The final third of the book brings hope, including the vision of a restored kingdom and an ideal temple.

Daniel is another book set during Judah's exile in Babylon. It offers a lively blend of dramatic narratives, profound prayers, and visions of future events. Daniel, with three Jewish companions, was taken captive in the first surrender of Jerusalem to the Chaldean invaders. The men were then trained in Chaldean values, beliefs, and social structures to become leaders in the captive assimilation process. Rather than adapt, however, Daniel and his companions managed to retain their vital devotion to Yahweh and carried their faith in God to the highest circles of Chaldean and Persian society. In the meantime, Daniel faced a number of challenges because of his faith, including an overnight stay in an execution chamber filled with lions. He was also invited to a banquet to interpret divine handwriting on a wall—the handwriting anticipated the Chaldean surrender to the Medes and Persians. Other foretelling aspects of Daniel, such as the emergence of Alexander the Great, proved to be so accurate that modern skeptics are convinced the book was composed after the fact—despite recent archaeological evidence that the book was, indeed, composed in Daniel's era. Readers will do well to view Daniel as a study in faithfulness, portraying a man who remains fully devoted to God even in the midst of the various allurements of his high political and social roles.

Hosea—the first of the collection of minor prophets that, together, complete the Old Testament is the shocking story of a prophet called by God to marry into a tragedy. Gomer, Hosea's wife, was either (depending on how the Hebrew text is read) the daughter of a prostitute who then became a prostitute herself, or a practicing prostitute when Hosea married her. Either way, the marriage ended in divorce because of her infidelity, and then the two became remarried on the basis of pure compassion. All this is done at God's bidding in order to display, in human terms, what God's relationship with the northern kingdom of Israel (also referred to as Ephraim) was like: God, though he will punish unfaithfulness, still maintains his love and covenant devotion for his chosen people. Readers will be surprised at the depth of God's passion and character in this book.

Joel is a book written at two levels, the first being the literal and immediate, while the second is the spiritual and prophetic. The immediate issues are the twin tragedies of a locust plague and a severe drought. The greater concern of the prophet, however, is the coming "Day of the Lord" that will be like the locust plague in its complete devastation of the land. In the face of such a threat the people are called to repent and to look to their compassionate God for restoration. In the prophecy Joel spoke of a coming day when God will send his Spirit and a day when the nations will be judged.

Amos, a prophet from Judah, was sent north by God to warn the kingdom of Israel to repent and to begin to seek God once again. His message begins with a series of promised judgments against the nations surrounding Israel, then moves to Israel herself. The message wasn't well received; Amos was told to go back to Judah. Amos himself was dismayed at the news of a set of possible judgments, and in each case, he pleaded for God's mercy to intervene. Finally God showed Amos a plumb line, perhaps indicating the role Amos was fulfilling to Israel, which showed Israel to be out of line. So, then, judgment was unavoidable, but God promised a future restoration as well.

Obadiah, on God's behalf, charged the nation of Edom (the present region of southern Jordan), whose father was Esau (see Genesis 27-36), with unwarranted hostility toward "your brother Jacob" (verse 10). When Jerusalem was attacked by a foreign army—probably the Chaldeans—the Edomites proved to be treacherous to their neighbors, siding with the foreign invaders rather than with their brother nation. God promised that their evil conduct would come back on their own heads.

Jonah, which tells the famous account of Jonah's being swallowed by a whale (actually "a great fish"), is the summary of a recalcitrant prophet who was sent to warn the people of Nineveh, the capital city of Assyria, about God's coming judgment. Jonah, perhaps anticipating the future devastation brought against Israel by Assyria, boarded a ship to flee from God and rejected his calling. This led to his adventure with the fish. God thus compelled him to get back on track and fulfill his preaching ministry in Assyria. As a result the city of Nineveh repented, to Jonah's dismay. The book discloses God's concern for the nations of the world.

Micah, a prophet of the same period as Amos, Hosea, and Isaiah, was another of the voices alerting the divided kingdoms of Israel that God's patience with their arrogant idolatry and immorality was running out. The wealthy princes and judges of both capital cities, Samaria in the north and Jerusalem in the south, were corrupt, abusing and demeaning the poorer people under them. The abuses involved prophets, too, as many of them promised peace rather than judgment. Consequently, Assyria was coming to bring destruction. Amid Micah's warnings, however, was the promise of a better day coming sometime after the judgment—Jerusalem would be eternally established under a king who would be born in the city of Bethlehem, the family city of King David.

Nahum promises the collapse of Nineveh, capital of Assyria. The former day of repentance brought about under Jonah's ministry had long since passed. God gave Nahum a distinctive vision of the fall of the proud city in graphic terms. Verbal pictures of clattering chariots, flashing swords, and pleading women give a sense of the horror of the invasion. The prophecy was a reminder that the nation used by God to punish Israel would later be punished for her godlessness.

Habakkuk ranks with the book of Job as an exposition of God's sovereignty and the problem of evil. Judah, having survived the Assyrian invasion (by God's intervention to save Jerusalem), still failed to embrace God wholeheartedly. Habakkuk, seeing sin all around him in Judah, entered into a dialogue with God, which we could paraphrase as follows: "Why, God, all this evil, when you are so pure?" God: "Don't worry; I'll use the Chaldeans to destroy your nation and solve the problem." Habakkuk: "God, that's overkill—the Chaldeans are worse than we are!" God: "Really? Are you sure?" At the heart of the book is a statement by God that anchors the theology of the New Testament: "The righteous will live by his faith" (see Romans 1:17). With that warning Habakkuk, by faith, accepted God's coming judgment as just but asked for mercy in it.

Zephaniah was dismayed by the same evil abuses in Judah that Habakkuk cited to God. Under God's direction, Zephaniah borrowed the same motif against Judah that was used by Joel to warn her northern sister, Israel: "Beware the coming day of the Lord." The people in

Zephaniah's day viewed God as impotent but their arrogance was simply a prelude to doom. Other nations were warned as well. God promised, however, that a remnant would survive his wrath because they belonged to him.

Haggai is the prophetic companion of Ezra. The restoration of the remnant of Judah after their captivity in Babylon opened the door for the Jews to reestablish their temple worship. The temple, however, needed to be rebuilt after its destruction by the Chaldean invaders more than 70 years earlier. Political pressures, cited in Ezra 4, stalled the first restoration effort. In the meantime, the exiles became more interested in setting up their own homes and economic affairs than in finishing the temple. Haggai told the people how God felt about that. His sharp, short message successfully rekindled the effort to rebuild the temple (see Ezra 5), which was then brought to completion.

Zechariah wrote during the time of the temple's reconstruction. His cryptic visions addressed the immediate circumstances of the remnant nation of Jews as they struggled to reestablish themselves in Israel. They also looked ahead to days of future tragedy and subsequent restoration. A major thread in his visions was the coming "Branch" who would rule as Priest and King. This anticipation of Christ included both his suffering and his exaltation—and it predicted his return to Jerusalem, coming down from heaven to stand on the Mount of Olives in Jerusalem. From then on the King would rule not only Jerusalem, but all the nations.

Malachi offers a picture of God's emotions as he confronted the newly restored Jewish society in Israel. Rather than live in awe and love, given God's care for them, the people, and the religious leaders in particular, were arrogant. Sacrificial ceremonies at the recently restored temple weren't being taken seriously. "Where," God thunders, "is someone ready to stop all this?!" Malachi's message came in the form of a disputation in which God's charges were answered by the defensive questions of the people: "Who, us?" Once again the "Day of Yahweh" motif emerges with a warning that in the coming day the wicked and the righteous would once again be distinguished with judgment brought on the one and joy on the other.

The New Testament

Matthew is the first of the three Synoptic Gospels—Matthew, Mark, and Luke—that share much the same form and content. Many see Mark as the first work, which was then used as a foundation for enlargements by Matthew and Luke. John, by comparison, is largely a unique and complementary account.

Matthew's message, while apparently incorporating most of Mark's account, was uniquely fashioned around five of Jesus' messages, which all end with a basic formula: "It came about when Jesus finished these sayings..." Evidently Matthew's audience was more Jewish in heritage than the audiences of the other Gospels because he often included statements about Jesus "fulfilling" the Old Testament Scriptures and because he addressed certain issues in greater detail that would be appreciated by Jewish Christians. The Gospel collection of messages, the flow, and the moral emphases make Matthew an excellent starting point for reading about the life of Christ.

Mark, by contrast to Matthew, feels a bit more hurried as it races from event to event in Christ's ministry. Papias, a very early church historian, attributed Mark's knowledge of Christ's life to the apostle Peter—and, indeed, it seems to be viewed from Peter's perspective at many points. This Gospel is blunt, activity-centered, relatively brief, and ends abruptly (which later writers tried to remedy by offering their own endings). It develops in stages, featuring the training of the apostles as Christ's future emissaries. Their chief task was to come to grips with Christ's identity, a matter they grasped in principle but without understanding its implications. Peter, for instance, confessed Jesus as the Christ, only to be rebuked immediately afterwards for trying to impose on Jesus his expectations of what that entailed.

Luke, the physician and companion of Paul, began his Gospel by noting his research of the events of Christ's life. Luke clearly drew from Mark's Gospel, and possibly Matthew's, too, but he also included a number of unique elements. Luke was especially alert to Christ's work of reconciliation—in a story unique to his Gospel, the tax-collector Zaccheus was called out of a tree by Jesus. Luke summarized the event with an editorial cue: "For the Son of Man has come to seek and to save that which was lost" (Luke 19:10). Luke's attention to detail and his addition of a number of events in Christ's life—including the figures of Simeon and Anna in chapter 2, the men Jesus met on the road to Emmaus, and the ascension from the Mount of Olives—serve to enrich the Gospel tradition and make this work a good "cap" to reading through the Synoptics.

John wrote his own memories of Christ in a captivating and theologically astute fashion. His goal was overt: "These have been written that you may believe that Jesus is the Christ, the Son of God; and that believing you may have life in His name" (John 20:31). John wove together a set of "signs" and discourses by Jesus in a manner calling for a decision of faith. The signs began with the relatively modest transformation of water into wine, then continued forward with various healings, including that of a man born blind, and concluded with a compelling miracle—the resurrection of Lazarus. These events polarized observers; religious leaders viewed Jesus as a threat, while the crowds saw him as a potential king.

In the end, only the disciples grasped Christ's purpose to die on behalf of many in order to grant them life. Over a third of the Gospel centers on the week leading to the crucifixion, with the Upper Room Discourse offering primary insights for Christians about the inner-workings of the Trinity and the ministry of the Spirit to Christ's disciples.

Acts, or the "Acts of the Apostles," is the second part of Luke's writings. It begins at the ascension of Christ and chronicles the journeys and imprisonment of Paul and his ministry in Rome. During this three-decade period the young church blossomed from a group of hesitant and shaken disciples to a major spiritual force in the Mediterranean basin. The key to this growth was the Spirit's work of transforming the new believers. Luke was careful to show that the relationship the disciples had with Christ, when stirred by the presence of the Spirit, caused the church to grow dramatically. Midway through Acts Paul was converted, and from there onward his missionary travels dominate the narrative. Luke joined Paul on a journey to Jerusalem, which began at Corinth and continued through Miletus. Paul's purpose was to aid the struggling Jewish Christians with a large financial gift from Gentile Christians. Then Paul was arrested and eventually shipped to Rome with Luke as one of his companions. This lively story of courageous Christian outreach is a powerful guide for growing in faith.

Romans is the backbone of the Bible in addressing matters of sin and salvation. Paul explains a symmetry of sin and grace, with grace always greater than our sin. Faith, which justifies the believer—making us righteous before God—is a work of God's grace in us, and also the means by which we live our new life in Christ. Sin is viewed as more than a set of flawed behaviors; instead, Paul portrays it as worshiping and serving the "creature" rather than the creator. Behaviors are linked to motives, and no one is motivated to seek God until the transforming work of the Holy Spirit captures us. Yet even with this work of making us one with Christ's death and resurrection, Christians will struggle until God completes his transformation in us by granting us resurrection bodies. Paul also explains God's work among the Jews, and he offers some ethical directions, defined by love, to provide paths for growing in faith.

1 Corinthians is a potent letter from Paul to the struggling young Christians in Corinth, a city famous for its debauchery. Paul addressed a list of divisive problems he was alerted to by "Chloe's household." These fissures in the church were the result of, among other things, an arrogant pseudowisdom, an abuse of grace linked to immoral license, and a selfish pseudospirituality. Paul wrote stern warnings against each of the abuses and exhorted the church to put its house in order. This called for ending personality-based divisions; for taking steps to confront some overt immorality; for establishing proper discipline in approaching the Lord's supper; and for regaining a healthy use (guided by love) of all the spiritual gifts rather than becoming fixated on the selfish use of tongues. All of Paul's concerns were anchored by the certainty of Christ's true gospel, which was validated by his death-defeating resurrection.

2 Corinthians is another letter from Paul to the Christians in Corinth, not unlike the first. The letter, however, begins with a positive set of personal reassurances and encouragements. In chapters 3–5, for instance, he offered a dramatic comparison of the superiority of the new era of the Spirit which magnifies Christ, over the law-centered era of Moses. The latter had a fading glory; the other had an increasing and intrinsic glory being displayed in transformed believers. This intrinsic work of God, modeled by Paul amid his persecutions, is a preparation for eternal glory with Christ. Thus, in this life, we are to be motivated by Christ's love. The tone of the letter shifts after this, becoming very stern at points. A major concern for Paul was that the church be prepared to help in the financial gift being collected for the struggling Christians in Jerusalem (see Acts). Paul was also aware that some in Corinth were questioning his authority, a matter he addressed forcefully near the end of the letter.

Galatians, also written by Paul, sets out a polarity between the use of the law for salvation and sanctification, and a life centered on Christ and lived by faith through the Spirit's intrinsic transformation. Paul was forced to defend his personal authority and the authority of his message against those who insisted on a law-centered spirituality: "You foolish Galatians!" he growled. "After beginning with the Spirit, are you now trying to attain your goal by human effort?" (Galatians 3:1,3 NIV). To return to the Old Testament law, Paul argued, was like Abraham's attempt to assist God in keeping a vow (that Abraham would have an heir) by Abraham's use of Hagar, his wife's maid, for that purpose. The fruit of that relationship was a "slave" (a son born to the slave), versus the true son (of Sarah, the true wife). So, too, attempting to live under the law is a renewal of fruitless enslavement; instead, we are to live by the Spirit.

Ephesians was written by Paul as a foundation-building letter for the young churches of Asia Minor (modern western Turkey). It was carried by Tychicus to these churches, which had been birthed by converts of Paul's ministry in Ephesus. The letter establishes some basic truths (chapters 1–3) and practices (chapters 4–6) of the faith. The context for Paul's message is his status as a Roman prisoner. This resulted from a false charge that he escorted Trophimus, an Ephesian friend and non-Jew, past a "Jews Only" dividing wall in the Temple courtyard of Jerusalem (see Acts 21). In Christ, Paul explained, there was no division between Jews and non-Jews; the debris of the old "dividing wall" must become the construction material of a new, inclusive temple, namely the church of Christ. In this building God's Spirit gives each person a unique function. Paul's "gift" from God is to spread this truth to all people; all others are to live with a sense of obligation and opportunity to live out their own function. Paul delineates many of the implications of these truths in the second half of the book, calling for transformed conduct. He offers special instructions about family relationships, pointing to marriage as a workshop for understanding the proper love relationship of Christ and the church.

Philippians is Paul's thank-you note to the church at Philippi, and a commendation of Timothy and Epaphroditus, who, it seems, were being sent by Paul to help deal with some internal squabbles in the church. The latter messenger was probably the source of news to Paul that tensions were present among some of the church members—including Euodia and Syntyche. While the problems weren't detailed in the letter, Paul called for some attitudes to change. Selfishness, grumbling, and contentiousness are condemned. Christ, by sharp contrast, is elevated as the model of selflessness. Paul's personal expressions of devotion to Christ are inviting and make this one of the most warmhearted and encouraging books of the Bible.

Colossians is similar to Ephesians: both were carried from Paul to their destinations by Tychicus, both offered exhortations to a new identity in Christ, and each called for transformed relationships in families and at the workplace. Colossae, however, had a problem with false teachings that threatened to undermine Christ's status in the eyes of the Colossians. Paul wrote to correct the "empty deception" of certain teachers. These teachers were promoting a special knowledge of "elementary principles," combined with undue attention to angelic forces and ascetic restrictions. Christ, Paul reminded them, is the creator and sustainer of the universe, the sole object of true worship, and the conqueror of all other spiritual forces, including any spiritual forces being promoted by the false teachers. Thus Paul's work to correct an error provides us with one of the Bible's clearest descriptions of Christ's greatness.

1 Thessalonians is Paul's response to a report from Timothy that the recently planted church in Thessalonica is growing despite some persecution. Paul, earlier, had been forced to leave the city prematurely because of hostility from anti-Christians (see Acts 17) and was concerned about the church's spiritual well-being. Timothy's report was positive except for a mention of some anxiety among the Thessalonians about the status of believers who had died before Christ's return. Paul reassured the living believers that those who had already died would not be disadvantaged when the day of the Lord's return finally arrived. He went on to encourage them to live in anticipation of that coming day, with lives transformed in light of their future "together with him."

2 Thessalonians reflects a continued uncertainty among local church members about the day of the Lord's return—the matter addressed in Paul's first letter. Someone had distorted Paul's teaching, claiming the day had come already. Paul wrote to reassure the believers that certain events had to precede Christ's return. The most prominent of these is the emergence of a "man of lawlessness" who will flourish through flagrant deceptions. The Thessalonians were called to stand firm in Christ's love. Some in the church, taking Christ's return to be so imminent that they quit work (and began to rely on others for food), were called to return to responsible employment.

1 Timothy, Paul's letter to his younger colleague who was helping guide the church in Ephesus, is rich with instructions about proper standards for church leadership. Timothy seems in need of reinforcement and the letter may not only be Paul's attempt to coach him, but a document meant to support Timothy in any disputes that might arise in the church. The qualifications and responsibilities of elders, deacons, and the behavior of women are central concerns.

2 Timothy is Paul's more personal letter to Timothy and reflects a very different set of circumstances than those of 1 Timothy. Here Paul was in prison and was aware that his life might soon end. Paul wanted to be certain that the transmission of the gospel was well cared for, even in the face of apostasy and opposition. He urged Timothy toward greater moral and spiritual purity; in particular Timothy was to hold fast to the Scriptures, which are God's provision for maintaining the health of the church.

Titus, another of Paul's students in ministry, was given instructions for establishing leaders for the church at Crete. Holding to the standards for eldership would be crucial to setting a good foundation. The decayed culture of Crete posed special challenges for the young Christians on the island, and Paul offered a set of guidelines for proper relationships and godly living.

Philemon is a letter that accompanied the return of a runaway slave to his master in Colossae (see Colossians 4:7-9). Philemon, the owner, was a member of the church in Colossae, and Onesimus, the slave, had become a Christian under Paul's care. Paul sent Onesimus back to Philemon, satisfying legal demands (and calling for the forgiveness of money stolen in the process), but he wanted Philemon to do even more. The help Onesimus provided to Paul, who was imprisoned at the time, was so important that Paul asked for Philemon to release the slave so he could return to him. The brief note is full of tact and affection.

Hebrews is of uncertain authorship (Tertullian attributed it to Barnabas) but of rich theological benefit. The needs of an audience of Jewish Christians defines the content. Some of the readers were still devoted to their Jewish religious heritage and simply wanted to embed their view of Jesus into an ongoing Judaism. Others understood that the coming of Jesus changed everything. The author supported the latter group, making a case of the superiority of Christ to any of the former religious responsibilities under Judaism. Jesus, he said, was the exact representation of God's nature in human form; he was the victor over death and the devil; the new and perpetual high priest of God; and the sacrifice for all the sins of those who are saved. The author repeatedly urged the readers not to fall away from their opportunity, but to embrace Christ for who he was, the author and finisher of the faith.

James, the half-brother of Jesus (see Acts 12:2,17; 15:13; Galatians 1:19), wrote about the applied side of faith, calling for Christians to engage in the full ethical dimensions of their new birth in Christ. James identified problems in the church—of favoritism toward the wealthy, lawsuits among believers, and hypocritical attitudes. James called Christians, instead, to the spiritual wisdom inherent in true faith; and to a true devotion to others. Heaven, and not this world, was to be the goal of a living faith.

1 Peter is a letter of encouragement meant for new converts. It coaches readers in the development of their new birth in Christ. Peter recognized the tension between the remnants of old ways and the impulses of God's work within, a work of the Word of God bearing fruit. The exhortations in the letter presumed some difficulties present among the readers, including persecution by non-believers and ethical carelessness by believers. Christ's example is offered as a moral guide, and his care as a source of encouragement.

2 Peter instructs and exhorts Christians who are being troubled by false teachers, cynics, and morally degraded participants in the Christian community. The letter offers principles for discriminating the real from the false, including distinctions between true prophets and false, genuine freedom in Christ and the immoral freedoms of license, and a true outlook on the future versus a cynical indifference to prophetic warnings.

1 John addresses a split in an unnamed church. Some of the members, influenced by leaders who claimed a special knowledge of God's will, left the main body and were trying to recruit others to join them. John confronted the claims of the false leaders and reassured the faithful members in the church of the certainty of their own standing with God. The reality of their faith was displayed by their love for God and for each other; by their ability to resist the false teaching and the improper conduct that came with it; and by their experience of the Spirit within them, who affirmed their love and their proper commitment to the truth.

2 & 3 John are a pair of short exhortations sent to leading members of small churches to deal with questions about itinerant teachers. One letter confronts the inappropriate hospitality offered to such teachers, while the other letter confronts an inappropriate *lack* of hospitality. In 2 John the church hosted teachers whose views about Christ were flawed. This was to cease and the teachers were not to be welcomed again. In 3 John the opposite problem was present. Some of the Christians who visited the church attended by Gaius (the letter's recipient), were not given the hospitality normally offered to visiting Christians because Diotrephes, a self-centered man, forbade it. Diotrephes, however, was wrong, and the problem was to be remedied. Taken together, the twin letters teach that love must be guided by proper values.

Revelation has two sections: the first, in chapters 1–3, is a disclosure by Christ, through John, to the young churches of West Asia (part of modern Turkey) about their standing with him. The second section, from chapter 4 onward, is an apocalyptic vision meant to reassure believers of God's sovereign rule by revealing his plans for the consummation of history. The book is rich with symbolic imagery, which makes it remarkably vivid and somewhat difficult to interpret. There are those who see it as strictly symbolic—an epic expression of good versus evil; and there are others who hold it to be linked to history. In the latter view, some interpreters see the book as a summary of past events despite its claim to be a prophecy of future things; others see it as a dramatic unfolding of ongoing history, in which past and present events are to be traced; and still others see it as a promise of events to come in the last days.

In any of these views, there is still another question to be resolved. That is, given the clusters of judgments unveiled in the book, should the clusters be seen as varied descriptions of the same events, as somewhat overlapping events, or as distinct events? Such questions won't be answered definitively short of heaven because the book is intentionally cryptic. It stirs curiosity and invites closer scrutiny. Revelation, when taken together with Daniel, is used by some interpreters to explain a period of enormous trial yet to come; and a further coming of a 1,000-year reign by Christ, followed by a final rebellion and entrance into the eternal state. Whatever the correct view, the book ends with the promise of the tree of life once again fully available to those who have bowed their hearts in worshiping Christ. The problem of sin is ended once and forever.

Section D

The concept of Bible discipleship was first widely presented in Moody Monthly *magazine in January 1988. Here is the original article. It may be copied and used for personal and small group ministry and to invite others to the principles of* Discover the Power of the Bible.

Make This the Year

Reading through the Bible in 12 months, or even 12 weeks, is not just a good idea.
By R. N. Frost

Sam, a retired missionary, was planting a church on the coast of British Columbia north of Vancouver, and two of us on a summer mission were helping with the building construction. We ate breakfast with Sam each morning in his beachside cottage before starting work. On each occasion we managed to trigger a delightful discourse of biblical truth. As often as not he'd start with quotes from Genesis and end up in Revelation after touching down four or five times in between.

Sam's Bible knowledge amazed me. His Scripture awareness had penetrated all aspects of his life, not in a rote fashion, but in a way that seemed accessible and functional. When I asked how he gained it, he laughed. "I just read my Bible."

"How much reading—how do you approach it?"

"I try to get through it at least two or three times a year."

I almost dropped my coffee. He had been reading at that pace for most of his Christian life, about 50 years!

The challenge captured me. Within two months I finished my first Bible read-through. I was in awe of God's greatness, holiness, and redemptive love. I recognized the vast and singular strength of his personality projecting through the broad range of writers and books of the two Testaments. It was as if I had truly felt the beginnings of knowing God intimately.

Some years later I discovered that such intensive Bible reading would work as strongly with others as it had with me. John was my Army roommate. He was a believer, but lacked any muscle in his faith. One morning, before I went on duty, he complained that he was being badgered for his faith while I was somehow exempt.

"Johnny," I remember steaming, "it's because you don't stand for anything! You say you believe in God, but you never spend any time with him."

I asked him why he scarcely read his Bible. In fact, had he ever read the Bible through?

When I came back for lunch at noon, he was finishing Genesis; by that evening he had almost made it through Exodus. Soon he was carrying his Bible to work. At breaks he would read segments to his amazed military police friends. He finished reading the whole Bible by the end of the second month.

John not only gained new credibility with his friends (and ended the badgering), but also helped to stimulate the young-adults fellowship we attended. John decided to attend Bible college after the Army; encouraged by his example, six others did also. I later asked him about the impact of his Bible reading. "I fell in love with the Lord," he said.

I've since adopted a team-reading approach and have read through the Bible with almost a dozen partners. A few years ago in a church in Boise, Idaho, I suggested to a young man, {Way}, that we do a read-through. Within a month his life changed so much that others began to follow our model even though it was never promoted as a ministry activity.

Two weeks ago I began another team read-through. Chris, my partner, is a 19-year-old in the college ministry I lead. He grew up in a Christian home, but until six months ago was generally indifferent to spiritual concerns. After participating in an early-morning Bible study for five weeks, he asked for another study, and I proposed a read-through together.

The rules are simple. We selected a date for completing the project (in this case, four months from our commencement). We meet Tuesday morning for an hour. We chat for about 15 minutes and then begin to read verses that we've underlined in our reading for the week. Each of us has 15 minutes to review as much as he can— there's never enough time for all the verses. Then we share requests and pray. It may not sound dramatic, but it is the highlight of my week.

The Dynamics

The purpose is to read the Bible for flow in the same way we might read any good book: whenever the time offers itself. That way we look at a free evening or Saturday morning as a "chance" to read, not as a requirement, in order to meet the weekly increment. This past Thursday, for example, Chris read for five hours.

We read at a personal pace, so we scarcely ever read the same sections at the same time. This has never been a problem; in fact, it's useful because it gives a double exposure to every section of the Bible.

Underlining is essential. It helps our concentration and demonstrates our "homework" to each other. Thus, in our meetings we just read our selected passages to each other—there isn't any obligation to teach. We pick a completion date that will challenge us. A fast pace gives a better overview. It also helps us make better use of our discretionary time.

I encourage my first-time participants to skim sections that are repetitive or exceptionally technical, particularly in the Old Testament. They can pay closer attention the next time through.

What I call "Bible discipleship" can also be adapted. On occasions I've given new Christians a New Testament "sampler" (a Gospel, Acts, and epistles from each of the New Testament writers) to read through in their first months of faith. The principal concern is to train new believers who are in the hungry stage of new growth to read whole books of Scripture.

Some Questions

• *Isn't the Bible too diverse and complex for an untrained reader?* No, especially if a young Christian has a more mature believer to answer some of the basic questions that may arise. In our first exposures to learning anything, in school or on the job, we're usually confronted with complexity. Nevertheless, we begin to find principles that become points of reference for further understanding. The task of a teacher or helper is to direct the learner toward principles that give order to complexity. These kinds of principles or doctrines emerge naturally in the informal talks between partners.

• *What's the best age or ability level for this approach?* One junior-high youth pastor used this method to help 24 of his youth read the New Testament during the summer. He reserved a 20-minute "report" period during each Wednesday meeting when the students would share what they had underlined. Everyone finished on time and with enthusiasm.

I once had a partner with a reading disorder. I bought audiotapes of the Bible for him to listen to while he marked the verses that caught his attention on a printed text.

Another youth pastor is using Bible discipleship with his core high-schoolers. In 15 years as a youth pastor, he says it has proven to be the most effective means to move young people toward greater spiritual maturity.

I believe that Bible discipleship works because it's Christ's preferred approach. Jesus gave clear directions for his followers to "abide" in his Word (John 8:31). To accept his instruction at face value and to apply it through intensive Bible reading assures that Christians are given a direct exposure to Scripture, which is necessary for spiritual growth.

Nick and his family left for Asia as missionaries this past August. Years earlier Nick had become a Christian just when [Way] and I were starting our read-through, so he and [Way] began to meet also. Nick assumed that all Christians read through the Bible in this way. His continued appetite for Scripture led to formal theological training. He still has this avid appetite, and now it's overflowing to others.

Bible discipleship also demonstrates the love of Christ. We need to show new believers how our bonding into the body of Christ works. This happens when two people are joined in high-commitment fellowship through the shared, vigorous pursuit of God. When the partners meet together after having read substantial sections of the Bible in a week—realizing that the Spirit has been present to do his own "underlining" in their lives—there will be real growth in biblical love that expresses itself in personal vulnerability and accountability, prayer, and friendship.

Paul assured the Ephesian elders that they had been given the "whole will of God" (Acts 20:27) in his ministry to them. The Bible now serves as our access to God's will. In a survey of the Bible, the Christian begins to gain an overview that aids his study of any given text. In most instances the writers of the New Testament assumed that their readers had a knowledge of the Old Testament. It's important for contemporary Christians to be equipped to respond to that assumption.

Sam's mark on my life is eternal, not because of any exceptional wisdom, but because he was a channel of the living Word of God. Jesus told the woman at the well about the very principle that Sam shared with me: "Whoever drinks the water I give him will never thirst. Indeed, the water I give him will become in him a spring of water welling up to eternal life" (John 4:13). Isn't it time for us to read the Bible vigorously, steadily, and fully?